SUCCESSFUL
HOME CELL
GROUPS

SUCCESSFUL HOME CELL GROUPS

Dr. Paul Yonggi Cho

with Harold Hostetler

Logos International
Plainfield, New Jersey

SUCCESSFUL HOME CELL GROUPS
Copyright © 1981 by Logos International
All rights reserved
Printed in the United States of America
Library of Congress Catalog Card Number: 81-80025
International Standard Book Number: 0-88270-513-X
Logos International, Plainfield, NJ 07060

Preface
Why Home Cell Groups?

For years I have been traveling all over the world, sharing in seminars and conferences the story of the miracle that God has performed in our church in Seoul, Korea. From a little tent mission in the poor section of the city in 1958, we have grown to be the largest single congregation in the world.

To bring this about, however, God had to change me and my attitudes. The traditional models of church growth and leadership simply do not work on such a large scale. But God has a method that does work. He has a secret for success, and He wants every church to have it. He has given it to us so that we can share it with others.

The world today desperately needs the message of Jesus as Savior and Lord. Our churches and our cities need revival, not just from time to time but 365 days a year. I know that such revival is possible, because it is happening right now at our church, the Full Gospel Central Church. It is happening because I have applied the principles I am about to relate in the pages of this book.

God did not mean for me to keep this secret for success to myself. In fact, in 1976 He prompted me to found Church Growth International, so that I could spread the news and the knowledge of church growth principles to pastors and laymen all over the world. But only a limited number of people can attend the seminars. The information must be made available to many, many more Christians. These principles are not mine, they are God's, and He has given them to us so that all of us may benefit from them.

I believe church growth is going to be one of the major moves of the Holy Spirit in the 1980s. This book is concerned with church growth, although that is not its title or its main subject. Church growth is a byproduct. The real secret is home cell groups.

Many churches have been founded on personalities, yet today these churches are dying. I have visited some magnificent cathedrals where only a handful of believers continue to worship. Famous preachers have spoken from their pulpits, but the shepherds have passed away and the sheep have scattered. This should not be. Churches should not have to depend on a single strong pastor.

There is another way. Home cell groups give every church member an opportunity to participate in the ministry of his church and to bring revival to his own neighborhood. Our members have found this kind of involvement very rewarding, and evangelism has multiplied because of it.

But certain guidelines must be followed if home cell groups are to succeed. Church growth and evangelism are not automatic byproducts. A number of churches have tried and failed, because they disregarded certain basic principles.

By following the guidelines I have presented here, you can bring the miracles of home cell groups and church growth to your own congregation. As you read, ask the Holy Spirit what your role is to be. The results are limited only by a lack of openness to Him.

Dr. Paul Yonggi Cho, Pastor
Full Gospel Central Church
Seoul, Korea
November, 1980

Contents

SUCCESSFUL HOME CELL GROUPS

1

Personal Ambition: Key to Disaster

In 1961 I decided to build the largest church in Korea. At that time I thought I was doing it for God, but today I realize that really I was doing it out of my own personal ambition. That proved to be disaster. The Lord had to let me fail so that I would turn to Him in my need and allow Him to build His own church— in His own way.

At that time we had a church of 600 members, a church that I had started three years earlier. We had just moved from the original site of the "tent church" at Taejo Dong, a slum area of Seoul, to a better location in the Sodaemoon (or West Gate) area of downtown. It was a growing church, and I was proud of the work I had accomplished in only three years. In fact, I had become too confident. If I could get 600 members in only three years, I reasoned, why could I not build the largest church in the city?

In those days the Yong Nak Presbyterian Church was the largest church in Seoul. It had about 6,000 members, and that proved to be a great challenge to me. In fact, one day, without anyone else knowing about it, I took a measuring stick and went over to the Presbyterian church in order to take its exact measurements. I determined the length and the width of the building, and I counted the number of pews. It seated more than 2,000 persons.

In my ambition, I then said, "I will build a church larger than this, and the Lord will fill it."

Early in my ministry God showed me the importance of setting goals and having faith to believe He would provide the growth for which I dreamed. He taught me to pray specifically for my needs. And when He gave me a growing ministry, He taught me to visualize the numbers of people that would be coming to my church. As I prayed and meditated, the Holy Spirit confirmed to me, often through the Scriptures, that He would give me the number of members I had requested.

The first year I asked God for 150 members, and I got 150 members. The second year I asked Him to double the membership, and I got 300 members. The third year I again asked him to double the membership, and by the end of that year we did have 600 members.

This time I decided to ask the Lord for five times as many members as we had, and to give them to us within three years. That would give our church 3,000 members by 1964—that was the number for which I felt I had the faith to believe.

As I prayed, I received confirmation that, indeed, God would build a church through me larger than the Yong Nak Presbyterian Church. I was excited! I did not wait for any further revelation on how the Lord wanted me to accomplish this; I simply began to work all the harder to bring in new members.

I thought God approved of what I was doing. After all, He was blessing our work with miracles and healings; that was what brought the people to the church. But I was convinced that God had made Yonggi Cho somebody special. He was doing all this work through *me!* Without me, nothing happened in the church.

After moving the church from its original site, where it had been known as the Taejo Dong Full Gospel Church, we renamed it Full Gospel Central Church. I was the pastor. I was the administrator. I was in charge of the Sunday school program. And, yes, oftentimes I was even the janitor. Full Gospel Central Church simply could not function without the Reverend Paul Yonggi Cho, I thought. I was the pivot around which the whole church revolved.

This was not an intentional thing with me. I had been raised during the Japanese occupation of Korea and had been forced to live in a very poverty-stricken situation. I had almost died from tuberculosis. As a response to my background, I had tremendous ambition to become famous and successful, and to make a lot of money. In fact, before I met Jesus Christ as my Savior, I had intended to become a physician.

So when I entered the ministry, in my heart there was a hidden goal to become a famous and successful preacher. I loved God and wanted to work for Him, but my hidden motive was always the drive to succeed. I was very egotistical, and I wanted to do everything my own way.

God had to destroy all that; otherwise the church would have been my work, not His. God had to break me so that I would be worthy to lead His flock. I did not know that at the time, and so in all of my striving for the Lord I was always running scared. Not only that, I was beginning to tire.

By 1964 we were behind schedule, compared with my request to God for 3,000 members. Our congregation had grown to 2,400, but I was already in big trouble. I still thought I was really accomplishing great things for the Lord, rushing around from early morning until late in the evening, but my nerves were beginning to wear out. I suffered from constant fatigue, yet I continued to force myself to keep the church moving. I preached, I counseled, I visited the sick, I knocked on doors—I was always on the move.

The crisis came one Sunday following the second morning service. We were scheduled to baptize 300 people. (According to our custom, we held believers' baptism only twice a year.) Dr. John Hurston, an American missionary who was helping me to pastor

4

the church, was there to assist me. However, because of the attitude I had developed, believing I had to do everything myself, I had told John I would baptize each new member personally. Considering myself a "specially chosen vessel of God," I thought God could bless these people only through me.

But John saw that I was already tired, as I went down into the water to receive the first member. "Cho, you'd better let me give you a hand," he said.

"No, no, I'm all right," I protested.

But I did not even dare think about the huge crowd of people waiting to be baptized. I took them one at a time, calling out, "I baptize you in the name of the Father, and of the Son, and of the Holy Spirit," as I lowered them into the water. Then, of course, I had to lift them out again.

I managed quite well with the first few people, but then came some ladies who were a little plump, and it really took a lot of effort for me to support them and lift them back out of the water. It was not long until I really began to feel the exhaustion, and I could feel the muscles in my arms begin to tremble.

At that point John Hurston said, "Cho, you look a little pale. Are you all right?"

"I'm okay," I said, nodding vigorously to emphasize my determination.

"No, I think you need to rest for a while," he persisted. "Come on out of the water and let me take over until you get your strength back."

"I told you I'm all right," I said firmly.

He nodded doubtfully. I knew he wasn't convinced. In my mind I asked the Lord to strengthen me.

To this day I don't know whether He actually did or whether I simply forced myself to stay on my feet through sheer willpower, but I held up through all 300 baptisms. By the time the last person left the water, I was dizzy and almost delirious.

Exhausted as I was, my work was not over. That afternoon I was scheduled to meet a visiting evangelist from the United States, and that evening I would be his interpreter.

Again John was concerned for my health, and he said to me, "You look so tired. Please rest this afternoon, and I'll go to the airport."

I shook my head. "He's expecting me," I said. I did not want to give up even one of my responsibilities as pastor.

So without even eating lunch, I drove out to the airport, greeted the evangelist and drove him to his hotel. All the while my legs were quivering whenever I stood up. Then I managed a short rest before I had to pick him up and drive him to the church.

At the beginning of the evening service some of the deacons joined John Hurston in expressing concern for my health. "Pastor Cho," one of them said, "you look so haggard. You cannot possibly interpret tonight. Let me go and find another interpreter."

But, I thought, who could interpret this man's

message instead of me? God's power was flowing through me, and I was the only one who could interpret properly.

"No, I will be all right," I assured them.

So the evangelist began to speak, and right away I knew I was in trouble. He was a typical fiery Pentecostal preacher, and he began to jump around and shout so much that, as an interpreter, I had a difficult time following him. He had the anointing, and I did not.

To compensate for my own lack of anointing, I began to try to put a little more expressiveness into my voice, and it was not long until I was shouting out the interpretation to every sentence. The evangelist glanced at me out of the corner of his eye, and then he, too, began to shriek and shout. Soon we were both shrieking and shouting, and jumping all around the podium.

By the time we were about a half hour into his message, I began to feel terrible cramps around my heart. I couldn't breathe. My knees were trembling. Finally my body could take no more and, against every effort of my will, I simply began to sag. Although I could still hear the evangelist shouting as my knees began to collapse, it seemed as though my eyes had suddenly been switched off. Everything went black.

As I was going down, I remember saying to God, "Lord, why are you punishing me publicly? You could have done this to me privately, in my office."

My eyes cleared as I lay there, and I looked up at John

and said, "John, I'm dying." My heart seemed to be trembling, and I struggled for breath—my whole system seemed to be crying out for oxygen. Finally I lost consciousness.

Meanwhile, the congregation was praying for me, but the visiting evangelist was left standing there at the podium, momentarily forgotten. Embarrassed, he simply looked on helplessly. There was nothing he could do; he had lost his mouthpiece.

When I regained consciousness, I struggled to my feet and feebly made my way back to the podium. The only thing I knew to do was dismiss the service, and I did. Then the deacons carried me out to an ambulance, and I was taken to the hospital.

In the emergency room I felt humiliated. I was the pastor who prayed for the sick, and the sick became well. What was I doing here? My ego simply could not accept it. I began to claim my healing; that's what I thought I was supposed to do. I expected the Lord to perform a miracle and send me home from the hospital.

"Take me out of this hospital," I cried. "I'm trusting the Word of God! By His stripes I am healed! I won't accept any injection. Don't give me any medicine."

The doctors finally gave up and the deacons drove me home.

But God was not ready to heal me. I continued to claim all the promises for healing in the Bible. If anybody ever claimed the Word of God, I did. I was a bachelor at the time, and I would sit up in my bed in my apartment and claim all of the Scriptures I could find concerning healing. I kept quoting them and quoting them, saying, "God, this is your promise. You *cannot* deny yourself! I claim it! In the name of Jesus, I'm healed!"

But I got no better. My heart continued to feel cramped, and I struggled to breathe. There were several doctors among the deacons of our church, and they offered to help, but I refused. "I'm standing on the Word of God," I said.

As I look back on that now, I realize I had only head faith at that time, not heart faith. Head faith cannot claim anything. I was claiming only the *logos,* which is the general Word of God. I have since learned that it is only when the Holy Spirit gives specific confirmation (*rhema,* the revealed Word of God to an individual) that we can claim any of those promises as our own. Then our faith becomes heart faith, and with that kind of faith we can move mountains.

I didn't know that then, so I just kept on claiming those promises, using head faith. I tried to ignore the symptoms. Never mind the fact that I couldn't even get out of bed. I tried to ignore the presence of death I sensed in my room. I would not give up.

The following Sunday I asked the deacons to take me to the church so that I could preach. I was so weak I couldn't leave the house for fear of fainting, and I needed a housekeeper to take care of me, but I still insisted on carrying out my responsibilities as pastor of the church. (In my absence, Dr. John Hurston and the woman who was to become my mother-in-law, the Rev. Jashil Choi, were carrying out many of the pastoral duties.)

After the deacons helped me to the podium, I stood in front of the anxious congregation. My body trembled all over. I began to preach in a very weak voice, speaking slowly and halting after every few sentences. I lasted for only eight minutes. Then I fainted.

The deacons took me to my office, and, when I awoke, I began to claim the promises of God again: "By His stripes I am healed. . . . He took my infirmities and carried away my sickness. . . ."

I tried to exercise blind faith, yet in my heart I had no confirmation from the Holy Spirit that I was going to be healed.

"Take me up to the second service," I told the deacons. "I am going to depend upon the Lord to give me strength."

At the second service I stood weakly at the podium and prayed, "Lord, now I am exercising faith, standing on your Word. Strengthen me."

This time I was able to preach for only five minutes before I fainted. Later, after the deacons took me home, I felt certain at last that I really was dying.

But then something happened within me. God seemed to be trying to reach me, telling me I couldn't just go on claiming all those promises blindly. I had never asked Him what His will was in my situation. In fact, until then I had never considered the possibility that God might choose not to heal me.

"Father," I said, "you gave all of these promises to us. But I claim them and you don't heal me. Aren't you going to heal me?"

Then I was startled by the very distinct voice of God: *"Son, I am going to heal you, but the healing is going to take ten years."*

It had not been an audible voice, but it was so clear that I knew I had not been mistaken. I was shaken. It was as though God had passed sentence on me, and yet there was a kind of peace in my trembling heart. I wanted to argue, but I knew I could not argue with God.

For the next ten years, from 1964 to 1974, I felt as though I were dying at every moment. It has become clear to me that an arrogant man pays a very high price—a hardened heart is very hard to break. I had wanted to be broken in an instant; instead it took ten years to destroy "the Great Cho," as I had come to consider myself.

It is difficult to describe the suffering I endured. Each morning when I woke up I would immediately feel my heart palpitating. There was a burning feeling of death that would begin to creep up from my toes, and I would say to myself, "Oh, I don't think I'm going to be able to make it today." But then I would think of God's promise to heal me, and I knew I was not going to die that day. So I would get out of bed, perspiring and dizzy and gasping for air, and take the medicine I now knew I needed.

My dream of having the largest church in Korea flashed before my eyes. How could I ever reach such a goal, I wondered, when I couldn't even pastor a church of 2,400 members?

But God said He was going to heal me, so I was not ready to give up. Even though I was too weak to stand at the podium and preach a sermon, I insisted that the deacons help me to the platform so that I could sit there while John Hurston preached.

As I continued on in this desperate state, I gradually became aware that God might have a higher purpose in my suffering, and I knew I needed to become more open to His leading. It was only then that He was able to begin unfolding His plan for me and for Full Gospel Central Church.

2

God's Reeducation Program

It was about a month after my collapse when God began to get through to me that I had been wrong in the methods I had been using to pastor our church.

I was flat on my back in my apartment. I was determined not to give up my ministry, yet I was completely unable to carry it out. John Hurston and Mrs. Choi were carrying the load, but with 2,400 members they were unable to minister to all of the needs of the people. John was not fluent in Korean, and therefore he was able to counsel and pray with very few of the members. Because Mrs. Choi was a woman, the men were reluctant to seek her counsel.

On top of that, Korea was still a poor country, and our members were having a difficult time paying the financial expenses of our growing congregation. Somehow I knew I needed to mobilize more people and get more lay members involved in the ministry of the church, but I didn't know how. Besides, I didn't know if asking them was justified.

In my state of exhaustion there didn't seem to be much that I could do. I was in bed most of the time, in and out of depression, feeling like a pile of broken junk. I couldn't leave my apartment unassisted for fear I might faint on the street.

I had fallen into the routine of napping and praying, napping and praying, fighting back at that feeling of creeping death and meditating on God's purpose in leaving me in this predicament. That led me into a number of intense Bible studies that were to prepare me for the time when God could begin to use me.

Before He could give me the full revelation, however, He took me through two preliminary Bible studies. The first was on divine healing. I had preached about divine healing with real conviction and had seen many people healed. Yet I seemed unable to muster the faith to be healed myself, and I realized I did not have a sound scriptural understanding of the topic.

The second subject was the need to have intimate fellowship with the Holy Spirit.

Both of these studies led me to write books. The first was entitled *Jesus Christ, the Divine Healer,* and the second was called simply *The Holy Spirit.* Through these studies I grew in my own faith and understanding. I found the study on the Holy Spirit especially revealing.

For instance, as I studied the Bible, I saw that, although we are told to have fellowship with the Father and with the Son we are to have "communion" with the Holy Spirit (2 Cor. 13:14). I learned that communion goes deeper than fellowship. One dictionary defines communion as "an intimate relationship with deep understanding," and another says it is "the act of sharing one's thoughts and emotions with another."

In my need, God spoke to me of the necessity for having communion with the Holy Spirit—to have intimate fellowship with Him, to share my deepest thoughts and emotions with Him.

"Think of a marriage," the Lord said to me. *"When a man marries a woman, he doesn't just bring her into his house and leave her there. He doesn't treat her as just a 'thing' in his house. No, he loves her and shares his life with her—intimately. That is the kind of relationship you are to have with the Holy Spirit."*

During the year from 1964 to 1965 I continued to be terribly ill, spending most of my time in bed, but during that time my fellowship with the Holy Spirit began to deepen and take on the characteristics of communion. I finished both of those books, and they went on to become best sellers in Korea, and later in Japan.

But those studies were only preliminary to the real revelation God wanted to give me. That revelation was to have the most powerful effect on my ministry Simply stated, the Lord wanted to show me that I needed to delegate responsibility in the church.

As I lay there on my bed, wondering how I would

ever again be able to manage the congregation of Full Gospel Central Church (let alone an even larger one), I asked the Holy Spirit, "Lord, what can I do?"

Suddenly I felt the Spirit speaking to my heart: *"Let my people go and grow."*

I was stunned and puzzled. What did that mean?

He continued, *"Let my people go from the kingdom of Yonggi Cho, but let them grow."*

"What do you mean, 'Let them grow'?" I asked.

"Help them to stand on their own feet. Help them to carry out ministry."

That made me really begin to search the Scriptures. I came to Paul's letter to the church at Ephesus, and that gave me courage. In Eph. 4:11 it said that God "gave some to be apostles, some to be prophets, some to be evangelists, and some to be pastors and teachers, to prepare God's people for works of service, so that the body of Christ may be built up" (NIV).

Then I saw it. God's servants (apostles, prophets, evangelists, pastors and teachers) are given to the Church to equip the lay people, so the lay people can carry out ministry, both inside and outside the Church.

Next I read in Acts 2:46-47 that there were two types of meetings in the early church. Not only did the disciples gather regularly at the Temple, but they also met together daily in their homes to break bread and to have fellowship.

I knew that in the early days of the Church there were 100,000 Christians in Jerusalem, out of a population of

200,000. Who could have taken care of all those people, since there were only twelve apostles? How could they take care of the house-to-house ministry? There had to be leaders of smaller groups—of house fellowships. Together with the seven deacons (Acts 6), the lay leaders would have had to share the responsibility of carrying out house-to-house ministry.

Until then my idea of the church was always a public building; I had never even considered the possibility of turning a house into a church. Yet the Bible clearly and specifically mentioned the church meeting in houses.

And I thought to myself, here I have been stressing only a temple ministry. We have no house-to-house ministry. I've just been telling our people to come to church on Sundays and Wednesdays. There is something we have been lacking.

My study carried me on to the sixth chapter of Acts, where the apostles chose seven deacons to minister to the physical needs of the growing congregation, while the apostles limited themselves to prayer and the preaching of the Word. But after the stoning of one of the deacons, Stephen, the church was scattered. Then even the deacons became preachers, as is evident from Philip's evangelism campaign to Samaria in Acts 8. The apostles had delegated not only the authority to minister to physical needs but also the authority to preach.

As I surveyed Acts, I saw that in addition to the 3,000 people added to the church on Pentecost, 5,000 more were added the following day. Yet there were only twelve apostles and seven deacons. Therefore, the only way for the believers to be taken care of in the house meetings was for each of those fellowships—or cell groups—to have a leader. The church, then, was well-organized to minister to the needs of a growing congregation.

"That's it!" I said to myself. It made sense. How else could the early church have absorbed 3,000 converts on the first day, when the Holy Spirit fell on the believers in the Upper Room on Pentecost? The needs of those people were taken care of in the homes, not in the Temple.

As I continued to read, I saw that other churches were mentioned as meeting in houses—the church in the house of Lydia (Acts 16:40), the church in the house of Priscilla and Aquilla (Rom. 16:3-5) and the church in the house of Philemon (Philem. 2). Clearly there was much scriptural support for home meetings.

Next I was drawn to Exodus 18 and Moses' struggles in trying to judge the Israelites in the wilderness. He would sit before them from mourning until night, listening to their disputes and judging their cases. His father-in-law, Jethro, saw that it was too much for him, and he showed Moses how to delegate authority so that he would not wear himself out trying to meet the needs of all those in his charge.

"But select capable men from all the people—men who fear God," Jethro told him, "trustworthy men who hate dishonest gain—and appoint them as officials over thousands, hundreds, fifties and tens. Have them serve as judges for the people at all times, but have them bring every difficult case to you; the simple cases they can decide themselves. That will make your load lighter, because they will share it with you" (Exod. 18:21-22, NIV).

I began to see that delegation of authority is definitely part of the will of God.

Gradually the idea began to form in my mind: Suppose I released my deacons to open their homes as house churches. Suppose they taught the people, prayed for them to be healed and helped them, and suppose the people helped one another in the same way in those home cell groups. The church could flourish in the homes, and the members could even evangelize by inviting their friends and neighbors to the meetings. Then on Sunday they could bring them to the church building for the worship service. That would exempt me from laboring in visiting and counseling, and other such time-consuming work. I would be free to be the pastor—to teach and preach and equip the lay leaders for ministry.

In the space of three weeks I had a whole new plan for our church. But I knew I would still have to get it accepted by the board of deacons, and I would have to make a good presentation—the deacons were already worried about my leadership.

Soon thereafter I was able to get up from my bed, but

I was still very weak and had to struggle to stay on my feet. I went to the doctor, who told me, "You have a very weak heart, and your whole system is very weak. You're suffering from nervous exhaustion, and the only advice I can give you is to give up the ministry. It's too much for you."

"Isn't there some medicine I can take?" I asked.

"No," he said. "There is actually nothing physically wrong with you. You have simply been working too hard. Your heart palpitations and your weakness are a reaction to overwork. The illness is strictly psychosomatic. I can't give you any medicine. It wouldn't do any good. You will have to find another profession that is less taxing on you emotionally."

It sounded like a death sentence to my ministry, but I was not willing to give up. God had promised to build a church through me, and He had promised to heal me, although the healing would take ten years. I would believe Him instead of the doctor.

3

Selling the Program to the Church

I was only twenty-eight years old, but my body was a wreck. The doctor had told me to give up preaching and choose some other profession. But despite the condition of my body, I felt tremendous excitement. God had spoken to me out of His Word during those days I lay on my bed. He had unveiled a whole plan to me for restructuring our church so that I would not have to carry the ministerial load alone. I was eager to put it into practice, because I was convinced it would work.

However, I could not simply go back to the church and order the members to implement the plan. Our church had 2,400 members, and it had a board of deacons that would have to approve any changes in the structure or in the ministry of the church.

"Lord, this is your plan," I prayed. "How can they fail to accept it, since it's your will?"

I was confident there would be no opposition.

A month after I was back on my feet, I called the deacon board together and said, "As you know, I am very sick, and I can't carry out all the work of the church, especially counseling and home visitation. And I cannot pray for the sick or even pray with people to be filled with the Holy Spirit."

I told them the things God had revealed to me in Scripture, and I said I was releasing them to carry out the ministry. I told them they needed to stand on their own feet. Then I presented the plan as God had given it to me. I showed the deacons how home cell meetings would work, and I laid out all of the scriptural support I had for this new system.

"Yes, you do have a good biblical argument," one of the deacons said. "This kind of arrangement would seem to be of the Lord. But we have not been trained to do the kinds of things you do. That's why we pay you to be our pastor."

"I am a busy man," said another deacon. "When I return home from work, I'm tired, and I need the privacy of my home. I would not be able to lead a home meeting."

There was not much other comment. Everyone basically agreed that the idea was scripturally sound, but they didn't see how it could work at Full Gospel Central Church. There seemed to be no way I could motivate them. No one got angry; they were simply convinced it couldn't be done.

After the meeting I began to have all sorts of doubts

about my ministry again. I was certain I knew what the deacons were thinking, even though they didn't express themselves during the meeting. They were thinking that they were paying me to do a job that I now was asking them to do for nothing. I began to fear that they would resent me for trying to maneuver them into doing my work, using my illness as an excuse.

The deacons seemed to have no compassion, I thought. No one had said anything about wanting a new pastor, but I began to hear some secondhand reports from members of the congregation that the deacons would not refuse my resignation if I should choose to submit it.

I was still extremely weak and subject to fainting spells, and the reaction of the deacons was a real setback. What was I to do? I sought out the one person in whom I had always felt I could confide, Mrs. Choi. I told her the whole story.

"We must seek the Lord on this," she said simply. "Let's pray together."

After a period of prayer and searching the Scriptures, Mrs. Choi and I were discussing the various alternatives to implementing the home cell group plan, and together we hit upon the idea of using the women of the church.

As we continued to pray about it, while I poured my heart out to the Lord, Mrs. Choi said, "I believe God has revealed this way to us because it is His way. I believe we should call the deaconesses together and present the plan to them."

I shook my head. How was this possible? Who would accept it? This was Seoul, Korea, not the United States. There is no feminist movement in Korea, for we have an Oriental culture that decisively puts women in a subordinate role throughout society For thousands of years Korean women have been subject to their husbands. Women have never done any big job, either in society or in the church. It was difficult for me even to think of delegating authority to women. How could they possibly lead home fellowship meetings? The men would rebel! Besides, didn't the Scriptures themselves say that women should keep silent in the church? That is what Paul had written in his letter to Timothy (1 Tim. 2:11).

As an Oriental, I had a special understanding of Paul's instruction to Timothy. Paul had been writing from an Oriental understanding. When I read his admonition that the women should keep silent, I related it to our own Korean society. In many churches in Korea it had been the custom to separate the men from the women in the worship services. The men would sit on the right as they entered the church, and the women would sit on the left. A large curtain was strung down the center aisle so that they could not even see one another.

But when a service was about to draw to a close, some of the overeager women would begin to whisper through the curtain to their husbands: "Are you there?

Are you ready to go? Meet me outside right after the service!" Sometimes the women would cause such a disturbance that the preacher would have to say, "Ladies, please keep silent until you are outside the church!"

And when Paul talked about Sarah calling Abraham "lord," I knew what that meant too. Even today in Oriental society, a wife will refer to her husband as her "lord." If she does not do that, she will have insulted him. If you ask a Korean woman how her husband's health is, she will reply, "My lord is well, thank you."

So, as I thought about using women in the church, all of these things were appearing in my mind, and I prayed, "God, you are really going to destroy our church with this kind of idea. If I ever tried to mobilize women and encouraged them to carry out the church business, the whole church would turn against me. All of Korean society would turn against me. I would be shut out completely."

Then the Lord distinctly answered me: *"Yes, that is your idea. My idea is to use the women."*

"Lord, if you really want me to use women, you'll have to prove it to me from Scripture," I said.

Then I went home. Because of my weakness, I had to get some rest.

During the next few days I constantly searched the Scriptures and asked God to reveal to me the verses that would support the use of women in the ministry. Gradually a new picture began to take shape. I began to see that Paul was not a male chauvinist after all. He frequently used women in his ministry, but only if they were under his authority. The literal translation of Rom. 16:1 calls Phoebe a deaconess of the church at Cenchrea; that means she had a responsible position in the church—but under Paul's authority. By his commending her to the church at Rome, it was clear he was commending her not just as a servant but as a preacher. Paul had delegated to her the authority to preach, and to me that meant she was free to minister.

Then in Rom. 16:3 Paul mentions Priscilla and Aquila and talks about the "church that is in their house" (verse 5). Who would the preacher have been in that house? Again I could draw on my Oriental background, because in the Oriental custom the leader is always mentioned first. The order in which Priscilla and Aquila were mentioned had nothing to do with "ladies before gentlemen." When a Westerner goes into the home of an Oriental, if he greets the wife before the husband, he is really bringing disgrace to that family. In fact, it is customary upon entering a Korean house, even when the husband is not at home, for the visitor to say to the wife first, "How is your husband?" Then the visitor is free to ask the wife, "How are you?" The husband always comes first; he is the head of the house.

Also in Korea we do not say, "Ladies and gentlemen." That would immediately cause trouble. Instead we say, "Gentlemen and ladies." In Korea the man does not stand back and hold open a door for a woman, but the woman waits and follows the man through the door. This is Oriental custom.

So when Paul talks about "Priscilla and Aquila," the order in which he mentions them must be judged against the Oriental culture in which he lived. Priscilla was the wife of Aquila, but when the Holy Spirit led Paul to mention Priscilla first, it means that Priscilla was the leader in the house church. Priscilla was the "pastor," as it were, and Aquila was the assistant, and she could pastor the home church because Paul had delegated his authority to her, not to Aquila.

Verse 6 says, "Greet Mary, who worked very hard for you" (NIV). Mary here is mentioned among the laborers for God, and that does not mean she was working in the kitchen, or changing children's diapers. The women Paul mentions were laboring together with him to preach the gospel! That includes Tryphena and Tryphosa, two women mentioned in verse 12, who are called "workers in the Lord" (NASB), not workers in the kitchen. In the same verse Paul mentions Persis, who "worked hard in the Lord."

How do people labor in the Lord? They do it by witnessing, praying with people, preaching and helping spiritually.

This showed me very clearly that God was using women in the New Testament, but it was always under a man's authority. For instance, Paul writes that when a woman prophesies (1 Cor. 11:5) she should have her head covered; otherwise she disgraces her head. That means women were free to prophesy, and prophecy is a form of preaching. But in their prophesying they had to demonstrate that they were under men's authority.

Then the Lord began to speak to me: *"Yonggi Cho, from whom was I born?"*

"From woman, Lord," I responded.

"And on whose lap was I nurtured?"

"Woman, Lord."

"And who followed me throughout my ministry and helped to meet my needs?"

"Women," I said.

"Who stayed until the last minutes of my crucifixion?"

"Women."

"And who came to anoint my body in the tomb?"

"The women."

"Who were the first witnesses to my resurrection?"

"The women."

"And to whom did I give the first message after my resurrection?"

"Mary Magdalene, a woman."

"To all of my questions you have answered, 'Woman.' Then why are you afraid of women? During my earthly ministry I was surrounded by dear, wonderful women. So why shouldn't my body, the Church, be surrounded and supported by women as well?"

What else could I do? The Lord had made it clear to me that it was His will to use women in the Church. The following week I called a meeting of the Women's

Missionary Association, and about twenty women, all deaconesses, waited to hear what I had to say. I explained the situation to them, telling them honestly about my health problems and explaining the revelation and the scriptural confirmation that Jashil Choi and I had received.

At the previous meeting of the deacons, the men had been so logical and rational in their responses, but here the women were compassionate. All of them were concerned about my health, and they unanimously agreed to follow my direction. Mrs. Choi accepted the responsibility for organizing the work, because I was too sick to do it. Under her direction, the city of Seoul was divided into twenty districts, corresponding to the number of women who had agreed to lead home cell meetings.

I did make one requirement of the women. I asked Mrs. Choi and all of the leaders to wear caps to signify they were under my authority, just as Paul had ordered that a woman must have her head covered when she prophesies. To everyone in the church it would indicate that the women were speaking not on their own authority but on mine.

I went back to my apartment that night, still as sick as ever, but with a wonderful feeling inside that God was doing something in our church. I was beginning to think that at last my worries were over.

Well, God *was* doing something in our church, but my troubles certainly had not come to an end. I had not been prepared for Satan's counterattack.

4

Satan's Counterattack:
the Seven Obstacles

On the Sunday after my meeting with the women, I unveiled the plan to the congregation. Again I went through the whole story of how the Lord had led me through the Scriptures to show us the need to establish home cell groups. I explained all of the verses that showed it was scriptural to delegate authority to women to lead these meetings.

"This is not my plan for the church, but it is God's plan," I emphasized. "Therefore, it is necessary for all of you to participate. The church is being divided into twenty districts, and each of you is to go to a district home cell meeting this week."

We handed out papers to everyone, showing them when and where their cell meetings were to be held.

Perhaps I was naive, but I actually thought most of the people would cooperate by attending the first meeting. I was wrong. There turned out to be a lot of opposition. Many argued that they didn't have time for an "extra meeting." The men protested about having to sit under the teaching of a woman, but I had expected that. What I had not expected was the reluctance of many of the women as well. After all, they said, hadn't they always been taught that it was the men who were in authority? They expected to be taught by men.

That first week it really seemed as though all hell were breaking out in my church, so strong did the rebellion appear. Of our 2,400 members, only about 400 to 600 attended the twenty neighborhood cell meetings. There were from twenty to thirty members in each meeting. No one seemed to know exactly what to expect or how to act, and the women leaders had to devise their own lessons to teach the groups. (I had given them no guidelines, simply because I did not have any guidelines to give them. I had made only two suggestions: Watch the Christians to see that they don't backslide, and go out and win your neighbors for Jesus Christ.)

The strongest objections came from the men, of course. They refused to allow a woman to lay hands on them for healing or to receive the baptism in the Holy Spirit. One woman was nearly beaten up by her husband for that. They also complained that the meetings were disorganized.

The following Sunday I emphasized even more strongly that the women were under *my* authority, and that they were speaking for *me* in the cell group meetings. That seemed to soothe many of the members, and after that those who were genuinely committed in their Christian faith submitted to the program. Of course, there were still quite a few cantankerous members who refused to have anything to do with the home cell groups. They tried to undermine the plan by urging others to stay away from the meetings. Many, I'm sure, felt I was trying to exert too much authority on the church.

The second week, attendance increased. Even though I had given no guidelines and was providing virtually no direct leadership, people were finding meaning in the meetings. But without direction, the women leaders were having great difficulty trying to find their own way. I was not prepared for some of the things they were doing.

For one thing, I had given the women no training to teach; I had not grounded them in sound doctrine. One leader did not even understand the doctrine of the Trinity, and she was teaching in her group that Christians worship three Gods: the Father, the Son and the Holy Ghost. She thought Jesus and the Holy Spirit were lesser Gods under the Father. Another taught that a person is not saved until he speaks in tongues. And a third leader said the form of baptism does not matter. (Our denomination prescribes water baptism by immersion.)

So the women were doing whatever they liked, and the whole church was in turmoil.

"Yes, just as I expected," I said. I was convinced that our church was about to be destroyed, just as I had told the Lord it would be.

Yet I heard the Holy Spirit gently speaking to me, saying, *"Yes, there is chaos, but remember that the whole earth was created out of chaos, and all good things come out of chaos. Stick with it."*

I found that some of the women actually were doing a very good job. They were going out into their neighborhoods and finding people who had some kind of need, and they were succeeding in bringing them into the cell groups and winning them to Christ. They organized good cell meetings and had a good service. I called these successful leaders into my office and asked them their secret. I found that those who were successful had had some kind of training.

"Pastor, you can't just release all of these women to lead and not give them any training," one of the women said to me. "You have to train them. You have delegated your authority to us. You should delegate your sermons too. You should not let any of us preach our own sermons."

I could see that she was right, and so that very day I began to write out my sermon notes and distribute them to the cell leaders. I called a meeting of all the leaders for every Wednesday, and at the meeting I would distribute the notes and explain them, and tell the women what I wanted them to teach. I even organized an order of worship for the cell meetings: There would be opening prayers and singing, followed by a representative (or corporate) prayer, preaching from the Word of God for encouragement (using my sermon outline), and then an offering. The meeting would end with testimonies, prayers for healing and the baptism in the Holy Spirit, and a closing prayer.

In less than a month after the start of home cell groups at Full Gospel Central Church, order was beginning to come to the meetings. I thought all the problems were solved. But they were not. One by one, six other major problems surfaced. Satan obviously was not willing for us to succeed without a fight, and he began to sow seeds for all kinds of obstacles to effective fellowship.

The second phase of problems occurred because of a lack of discipline. The cell meetings were growing, and the leaders were carrying out my program, teaching the Word, praying for needs and providing real fellowship, but they did not know when to stop. Soon the meetings took on the character of a party. Members would alternate as hosts, so that the meetings moved from house to house in each succeeding week. In one house the people would be treated to rice and *kimchi* (hot, spicy pickled vegetables), but the next week the new host would add fish to the menu, and the third week they would have steak. They began to compete with one another to show what good hosts they were.

But soon some of the people became discouraged and depressed, afraid to have a cell meeting in their homes because they could not afford to put out a fancier spread of food than the previous hosts.

In addition, these "party meetings" were lasting so long that wives were neglecting their household duties, and husbands were arriving late for work. The ministry and the message were being lost in all the partying. Finally I established another rule: The leaders were to follow the order of service I had prescribed, and they were to conclude the meeting in one hour. The meetings were to begin and end on time. Food should be limited to tea and cookies.

Things improved, but still the meetings lasted too long. The tea and cookies were served at the beginning of the meeting, and the leaders could never seem to begin and end on time. Finally, after about six months, I asked them to postpone the refreshments until the end of the meeting. That seemed to restore order.

But other problems continued to surface. Most of them were not big things, such as the initial problems of teaching and lack of discipline, and they did not affect all of the cell groups. But they were serious enough for me to take corrective action.

The third phase of problems involved outside speakers. From time to time the cell group leaders wanted to take advantage of visiting evangelists and others, and they would invite them to come to speak at the cell meetings. Most of those speakers had their own self-propagating ministries, and they would expect to receive an offering wherever they went. So the cell groups would take up an offering for each for them without consulting me or the board of deacons. In addition, I did not really know who was being invited, since no one ever consulted me, and I found that I did not agree with some of the teachings I heard were coming from those speakers.

The only thing I could do was tell the cell group leaders that they were not to invite outside speakers without first consulting me, and they were not to take up an offering for anything except the work of our church. Only the leaders were to do the teaching, basing their lessons on the outlines I distributed to them each week.

Although the problem of outside speakers was brought under control at that time, it still crops up every once in a while. Now, however, I have a system of checks and balances in the church, and such things do not go on without my knowledge.

Then came the fourth phase of troubles, and again it involved money. At some of the cell meetings members began to borrow money from one another, and some of them even charged interest! Not only that, but some members began to promote investment opportunities. So we had members investing money in businesses belonging to other members, and often they lost their whole investment because of poor business practices. That was another thing I had to stop, and so I did.

The fifth crisis in the development of home cell groups involved burgeoning attendance. As the cells began to grow, we had some groups with thirty to fifty families. During the meetings those members packed not only the living room and the bedrooms but they also spilled over into the yard. A single leader could not take care of all those people.

It was apparent something would have to be done to split the cells into smaller groups. So I worked out a plan to train assistant leaders for each fellowship, and then we divided the groups so that there would be no more than fifteen families in any one cell.

At first the families were reluctant to divide. Many of them had formed an attachment to the leader. But I told them that they had to understand the greater purpose of the cell groups, which was to evangelize the neighborhoods by providing a place to bring friends and neighbors so that they could be introduced to Jesus Christ.

Finally I had to make it an established rule: They must divide when the group exceeded fifteen families. It was not easy, but slowly the members showed more cooperation, although some of them would attend both the new subdivided cell and their old one, because they felt a loyalty to the leader. It really took quite some time until there was full cooperation.

The sixth phase of problems was a very embarrassing one. An offering was taken in each of the cell meetings, and sometimes the leaders were tempted to borrow from the collection, since they did not have to turn it in to the church until Sunday. However, not all of the money that had been "borrowed" found its way to the church treasurer.

When I found out about this, I knew it was time to bring a little more formal organization to the home cell groups. I appointed a registrar and a treasurer in each of the cells. When the offering was taken each week, the registrar had the responsibility of counting it and keeping a record, and the treasurer held on to the money until it was to be turned over to the treasurer on Sunday. That way I always had somebody checking to see that there was complete honesty.

By now I saw the need for strict organization and for a system of checks and balances, so I could keep track of what was happening in the cells. I made up an information sheet that had to be filled out by each cell leader following the weekly meeting. On it the leaders would record the name of the speaker, attendance, the number who were saved, the number who backslid and the amount of the offering. With that I began to be able to see more clearly the direction in which the home fellowships were moving.

In fact, organization became a necessity. The cells were growing so fast that Mrs. Choi could not keep up with all the work of administration. She was doing most of it because I was still too sick. The cells quickly increased to 150, and we decided it was time to hire some assistant ministers. We hired three of them, and we put fifty home cell groups under each licensed minister.

It may seem amazing that, despite the problems with my health and the problems with our church, there was any time for me to think about a wife. But I did. Mrs. Choi had a lovely daughter, Sung Hae Kim, who was a graduate of the Ewha Women's University, the largest Christian women's university in the world. She also was a talented musician, and she often performed in the church. I found myself very much attracted to her, and I was happy to learn eventually that the attraction was mutual. On March 1, 1965, we were married.

But I must confess that, although our marriage has been a very happy one, our wedding day was not a particularly good experience for me. I was still so sick, and I was afraid I might faint during the ceremony. I had to ask the Lord for special strength. I was very nervous.

There were more than 3,000 people in the church for the wedding, and we had asked a missionary to perform the ceremony. Seeing all those people made him very excited, and he really got carried away with his sermon. In fact, he preached for a whole hour while I and my bride just stood there. Oh, did I struggle not to faint! That's all I remember—standing there struggling to stand upright. I don't even remember reciting the marriage vows!

On our honeymoon my wife spent the whole time just taking care of me.

But at least I felt that most of the major problems with our home cell groups had been solved. The groups were really beginning to show the marks of success. Members were inviting their neighbors to the meetings, and these people were meeting the Lord Jesus Christ as their personal Savior. The cells were growing and dividing, and more people were being added to the church every week. As the number of cells increased, we hired more licensed ministers and appointed more deacons and deaconesses to watch over them.

Still, in my condition, I was unable to appreciate the growth of Full Gospel Central Church. We were not keeping membership records, and the last official count I recalled seeing was the 2,400 figure recorded in 1964. I knew we were much larger than that because of the number of home cell groups, but I could not bring myself to look at the church in terms of the exact number of members. In fact, I could hardly keep my mind on anything at all. My memory was so bad during those years that sometimes I couldn't even remember the names of my sons.

It seemed as though I was barely holding on to life. Every moment I felt I was at death's door. Every day I would say, "Lord, just let me preach one more sermon, and then I can die."

Even in that condition, God sent me out. The news was spreading about the growth that was taking place in our church. Not only was it well-known throughout Korea, but our denomination, the Assemblies of God,

41

was very excited about it too. I was appointed general superintendent for all of the Assembly of God churches in Seoul, and I served on the advisory committee to the Pentecostal World Conference, which was held in Brazil and Seoul.

In addition, our church was involved in a major missionary program, and I was helping to set up the home cell group programs on the mission field served by our missionaries.

So I soon found myself fainting in some very unexpected places. Once I fainted in the Tokyo airport. Another time I fainted in an Assembly of God church in the United States, and I also fainted at the denomination's headquarters in Springfield, Missouri. I found myself fainting in hotels and motels. My life was miserable.

But I continued praying for the sick, and many people were healed. Every time I witnessed a healing, I would silently plead with God, "Lord, me too, please. Me too!"

But God had said ten years, and ten years it was to be. During that whole time I suffered excruciating pain. I knew I was no longer in control of anything. How could I be, when I was so sick? Once I had wanted to be successful and important, and I wanted to have control of everything that happened in our church. I wanted to build the biggest church in Korea. But none of those things was important anymore. I had become totally dependent on the Lord for every day of my life, for every movement of my body, for every single breath I took—and God was merciful to me.

I realize now that God was breaking me during that period of my life. I now know it is very necessary for a leader to be broken. If he isn't broken, he will never be able to lead God's people as a shepherd leads the sheep, because he will always be leading out of fear. He will be thinking of money or of power, because he will be afraid of losing his authority or his position. He will never be able to put his trust in the lay people and delegate authority to them for fear of losing his own position and authority. He will be afraid that any mistake they make might reflect on him. He will do a lot of things *for* the Lord, but God will not be able to use him, because he will be afraid to listen.

God will use people only according to their brokenness. I know now that God really could not use me until I was completely broken, until I could no longer rely on my own strength. And so after ten years of suffering, I had become nothing more than dust. I was helpless.

Toward the end of those ten years our church received a vision to construct a new church building. It would be on the newly developed Yoido Island in the Han River, where new apartments and government buildings were under development. We acquired some land there, and the new building was completed in 1973.

It was only then that I finally discovered just how many people we had. When it came time to move, there were

18,000 members of Full Gospel Central Church, all of them involved in the home cell groups. But not all of them wanted to leave the old building in Sodaemoon. We made an agreement to allow 8,000 to stay there, and the denomination appointed a new pastor to take over that church. Then we moved to our new Full Gospel Central Church with 10,000 members. We were still smaller than the Yong Nak Presbyterian Church, but we were growing, and I knew the potential was virtually unlimited because of the open-ended system of cell groups.

The wonderful thing for me during that move was that the healing God had promised me finally became a reality. I cannot point to a particular day or hour, but slowly the healing that I knew would be mine began to seep into my heart, and my heart was completely healed. The palpitations stopped, and I gained new physical strength. No longer did I sense that feeling of impending death.

Even today, however, I cannot say I am completely healed. My mind still has a tendency, whenever I am exhausted, to go in many directions, and my memory fails. At times I still have difficulty remembering the names of some of my close associates. But the healing process is still going on in my body, and I am depending on God for everything. Now that "the Great Cho" is dead, I do not strive for money or fame or power, because all desire for those things has been taken from me. From my experience I realize those things are all like a big bubble that can burst at any moment.

Yet with the healing I still have one major problem facing me—the seventh and final major assault from Satan to try to break up our thriving church. But that problem did not develop for another couple of years.

The first year we were at the new church on Yoido Island we gained 3,000 members. I began to encourage the cell groups to seek more members by going throughout their neighborhoods and sharing the good news of what God had done for them. I began to set goals for each of the cells, and for each district that was made up of a group of cells. As I continued to dream of the members I expected to fill the new building, God gave me the confirmation *(rhema),* and I would claim the growth—year by year, and even month by month. After several years we were winning 3,000 souls a month for Christ.

When the seventh major assault from Satan came, it was one of the worst I could have imagined. It is one that the women of the church never would have considered. The women were with me 100 percent. But some of the men in leadership began to let their responsibilities and their authority go to their heads. Three of the licensed ministers (each of whom had fifty home cell groups under his authority) began to feel that the members were loyal to *them* rather than to me or the church

Those three licensed ministers decided to call their

flocks of fifty cells each to split off from Full Gospel Central Church, to form their own churches. These churches had the potential for being quite sizable because each of those ministers actually was overseeing 2,000 members.

I plainly told the men that I did not approve of what they were doing. They were stealing my sheep! But they refused to listen to me, and they sent word to everyone in the cell groups under them not to worship at Full Gospel Central Church any longer on Sunday mornings. Instead they would have their own worship services in their own districts of the city. Of course, I sent word to the cell groups that I did not approve of this division.

The "split" lasted for about six months. When the separate Sunday meetings began, each of the three licensed ministers discovered he had only 300 to 500 members, rather than the 2,000 or so each had expected. But they went ahead and continued to meet separately, considering themselves to be newly established churches.

In the meantime, to take care of the remaining members of our congregation in those districts, I appointed new licensed ministers over the cell groups that remained loyal to Full Gospel Central Church.

Then gradually the members who had left the church began to drift back. By the end of six months those three ministers had so few followers that they were forced to give up and leave the city. Each of them now has a small church elsewhere in Korea, but the Lord has not blessed them as they had envisioned in the beginning.

The mistake made by those men was in thinking that, because I had delegated my authority to them, the people actually were following them. They were wrong. The people were following me.

Since then I have taken some steps to provide for those who have ambition among the men of our church. If a home cell leader wants to become a licensed minister, I will pay for his tuition to go to Bible school, with the stipulation that, upon graduation, he spend at least three years as one of the licensed ministers of our church. After that, if he still wants to have a church of his own, I will help him. I will provide him with a salary and enough expense money to start his own church elsewhere. But it must be a church to bring in new members, not to take members away from the mother church.

So far, seventy-five churches and missionary works have been started by members of Full Gospel Central Church in just this manner. They are all over the world, including Japan, Australia, the United States, Latin America and Europe.

5

The Security of Cell Groups

One of the major problems of society today is the depersonalization of human beings. With the increases in population, everyone becomes just a face in the crowd. Many books have been written about the difficulties people are having trying to cope with this depersonalization, in which they see themselves only as numbers. They feel alienated, lonely, aimless.

This problem has also found its way into many of our churches, particularly the larger ones. Many of the dynamic larger churches have been built on the strong personal preaching ministry of an anointed man of God, whose teaching and encouragement are so needed by his parishioners. People are hungry for the Word of God and for the assurance that God considers them more than mere numbers. Yet while they are hearing words of encouragement from the pulpit, they are experiencing in church much the same thing as in secular life. They are merely spectators.

It is true that in many of these churches *some* of the members of the congregation are involved in a limited way in meaningful group activities and relationships. There are Bible studies and prayer groups, but usually only a small percentage of any congregation is involved in such groups. And sometimes in these groups there is little opportunity for personal involvement, particularly if the group is a formal Bible study class. The initial enthusiasm of new members gradually wears off, and eventually they become only Sunday Christians— even in some very "alive" churches.

Home cell groups, on the other hand, provide a real opportunity for people such as these to find meaningful involvement in the life of their church. Not everyone can be an elder or a deacon in a large church; not everyone can teach Sunday school or provide counseling. But with home cell groups there is an opportunity for everybody to become involved.

I like to describe Full Gospel Central Church as the smallest church in the world as well as the biggest church in the world. It is the biggest because, as of the writing of this book, our congregation numbers more than 150,000 people. But it is also the smallest church in the world—because every member is part of a home cell group consisting of fifteen families or fewer.

Each week these members gather in their neighborhood cell meetings, where they have an opportunity to worship the Lord, to pray together, to learn from the

Word, to experience the working of the gifts of the Holy Spirit, to see miracles and healings and to enjoy loving relationships with their fellow Christians. In the cell groups they are no longer numbers; they are people—individuals. A person who comes into the cell group discovers he is an "I" and not an it. The cell leader becomes a kind of pastor to him, although one who is responsible to the church. The cell leader knows each of the members of his group and can relate personally to their joys and problems with a kind of familiarity that a senior pastor cannot develop.

The Sunday services in our church are very structured, very traditional. The number of people in each service is usually about 15,000, and that limits the participation of each individual to the singing of hymns and to regulated times of congregational praise. Other than that, they are there to receive—to receive instruction from the message, to receive healing or assurance from the Lord. And they are there to enjoy the celebration and to give their offerings to God.

But in the home cell groups each one has an opportunity to be used by God to minister to the others in the group. The Bible says that the Holy Spirit distributes His gifts as He chooses (1 Cor. 12:11). In our cell groups, although the leader teaches from the Word of God, based on the church-approved outline, the other members have the opportunity to bring a word of prophecy, tongues and interpretation, a word of knowledge or a word of wisdom. Each member can pray for the sick and in faith believe God will hear his prayer and heal that person.

Above all, each person can become involved in the revival of his own neighborhood. I will discuss this in more detail in the next chapter, but let me say here that my members have found it extremely rewarding to share their love with unbelievers in their neighborhoods or in their apartment buildings, especially when the neighbors gladly accept an invitation to a home cell meeting. Every one of my members thus becomes a missionary to his own neighborhood and an agent for revival in that neighborhood.

The members of Full Gospel Central Church are enthusiastic. They are experiencing revival 365 days a year. Every church needs that kind of revival, and our members are experiencing it because they are actively involved in it.

No revival should be the product of a single personality. I do not claim to be responsible for the revival that is occurring in our church. In fact, the revival continues whether I am there or not, and at the present time I spend six months of the year traveling outside of Korea. The church experiences revival when I am not there because the Holy Spirit is able to use all of the members through the home cell groups. That means the revival will not die out after the span of my lifetime, not as long as the church adheres to the principles of home cell groups under the guidance of the Holy Spirit.

There is much security for the members in the cell

groups. Each one becomes a family member with the others of the group in a kind of community relationship that is more than a community. In the group each person is free to discuss his problems and seek counsel and prayer for them. In fact, the relationship goes beyond counsel and prayer; the members really take care of one another.

An illustration of just how much our members care for one another is the case of one family in which the husband has been out of work for a long time. The members of their cell group have helped to provide them with extra food from time to time, and even with necessary warm clothing. In fact, the group even took up a collection to help send one of this family's children to college!

Members of cell groups have gone to clean the houses of women in their group who have fallen ill. They have visited other members in the hospital, where they have prayed for healing and have brought tremendous encouragement. And when there is a death in the family of one of the members of the group, it is like a death in the cell group family; all of the members go to the aid of the family that experienced the loss, to mourn with them and to provide for their immediate needs.

It's a wonderful communal life. Each one is helping the other. When a member belongs to a home cell group, he knows he is loved and cared for, and that is the kind of security many people never find in churches that do not have cell groups.

The security in our home cell groups is increased because most of them are more than just neighborhood groups. They are even more specialized than that. Many of our groups are women's neighborhood groups. Because the men do most of the work in Korea, the women stay at home and look after the house and the children. They have time to meet during the day. Fifteen to twenty housewives will gather in the house or apartment of one of the members each week, and one of the women will be the leader.

The men usually work long hours, and they are often too tired to have a meeting during the week. So we have many men's cell meetings on Saturday nights, and these are led by the men. Of course, these groups are not limited to having only men or only women. Men oftentimes attend the women's groups, particularly if they have a day off during the week or are recuperating from an illness or injury; and the wives will sometimes go with their husbands to the Saturday-night meetings, even if they have already attended their own meetings during the week.

In addition we have youth meetings and children's meetings—all variations of the home cell group meeting but designed especially for the younger person.

We also have some very specialized meetings, such as those in offices and factories during the workday. In one area of the city where there was an unusually large concentration of secretaries, the women found that the best time for them to have a cell meeting was during their lunch hour. So they arranged a place in one of the office buildings, and each week they meet to study the Word of God and to have fellowship and prayer together. Not only that, but such a meeting is an ideal place for the women to invite a co-worker, because they have so much in common.

In another section of Seoul the workers in one of the city's largest chocolate factories decided that they too wanted a cell meeting during the workday. They went to the management and told them their desire, but at first the supervisors were reluctant, because they felt there was not enough time during the lunch period and they were afraid the employees would be late getting back to their jobs.

But the employees were not ready to give up. They prayed about it, and then they gave the manager a plan:

"Give us an extra hour after lunch for us to have our cell group meeting," the leader said, "and we will work an extra hour at the end of the day. We will still put in the required amount of work time, so that there will be no loss of production, and you will not have to pay us extra for the longer workday."

The manager was skeptical, but he decided to let them prove themselves. After a few weeks he was amazed. Not only were the workers from Full Gospel Central Church keeping their part of the bargain, but they actually were producing more chocolate per worker than the other employees. He was so pleased that he called up the church office and asked to speak to me.

"Pastor Cho, I cannot believe the zeal of your members!" he said. "They are the best workers in our factory. Please, if you have any more members such as these, send them to us. We will be happy to give them jobs!"

That really says something for the enthusiasm of the members of our church. I attribute all of this to cell groups. Our people are really excited, and that is the best form of evangelism we have.

6

Home Cell Groups: a Key to Evangelism

The human body needs to renew and replenish itself constantly or it will die. That requirement is just as true for the Church, the body of Christ. Therefore, one of the needs of a dynamic and growing church life is evangelism. If a church is not involved in serious evangelism, it will either remain stagnant or it will begin to die.

But more than that, it is the command of our Lord Jesus Christ to evangelize—to go into all the world and preach the gospel and make disciples.

When Jesus told His disciples that they would be His witnesses after the Holy Spirit came upon them, He said they would first be witnesses right there in their own hometown—in Jerusalem. It was only after they evangelized Jerusalem that they spread out into Judea and Samaria and, finally, to the ends of the earth.

Each of our churches needs to be involved in evan-

57

gelism like that. We need evangelism that begins right in our own neighborhoods, in our cities and villages, wherever the Lord has planted us. That is the kind of evangelism we practice at Full Gospel Central Church in Seoul, and that is the reason for the tremendous growth we have experienced.

But our church does not follow the familiar pattern of door-to-door evangelism. In many respects that is a confrontation type of evangelism; it invites resistance. It's the same kind of resistance that a Christian puts up when a member of the Jehovah's Witnesses or the Mormons calls on him. It's true that many people are saved through door-to-door Christian witnessing, and the Holy Spirit will sometimes motivate Christians to undertake that kind of evangelism in areas where He has already prepared the hearts of the unbelievers. But in general, door-to-door evangelism becomes frustrating for the Christian witness because he sees such a low rate of productivity.

Our church, however, carries out evangelism primarily through the home cell group system. Each cell group becomes a nucleus of revival in its neighborhood, because the cell group is where real *life* is to be found in that neighborhood. When a home cell meeting is full of life, and when people are happy and sharing their faith and witnessing to what the Lord has done in their lives, other people are drawn to them. Unbelievers become curious. They want to know why this little group of Christians is so joyful when all around them there are so many troubles.

Now, even though such groups become magnets in their neighborhoods, our members still have to work at evangelizing. Unbelievers infrequently come beating on the doors to find out what is happening. Our members have to go out looking for prospective converts. But we have other ways of helping them to become caring evangelists.

One way is through what we call "holy eavesdropping." Our cell leaders instruct the members of their group to be on the lookout for anyone who is having troubles. Many of us overhear conversations every day in which someone is speaking about the problems in his life. Whenever we overhear such conversations, we should immediately ask the Holy Spirit, "Is there some way I can witness to this person? Is there some way I can introduce him to Jesus, who can really solve his problems?"

In one case that was related to me, a woman from our congregation witnessed to a woman she had met at the neighborhood supermarket. She had overheard the woman, an unbeliever, telling a friend about problems with her marriage. She was on the verge of divorce. It turned out that our member had had some very similar problems, but the Lord Jesus had saved her marriage through prayer and through the ministry of the home fellowship.

Outside the market our member caught up with the other woman and said, "I couldn't help overhearing you discussing your problem with your friend. I had a very similar problem. Would you like to come over for tea while I tell you how I overcame that problem and saved my marriage?"

To her surprise, the woman accepted on the spot. During the time of sharing, our member told how she and her husband had been at the point of almost agreeing to a divorce, when they met the Lord and their lives were turned around. She did not immediately urge the woman to accept Christ as her Savior, but she did relate how much the home cell group meetings meant and invited the woman to the next one. She assured her that there were a lot of understanding neighborhood women in the group who would be able to identify with this woman's problems.

When she attended the cell meeting for the first time, the woman was immediately impressed. Although she did have a little difficulty with the enthusiastic singing, the hand-clapping and so on, she saw that the women were all much like she was. Yet there was a serenity about them that she longed to have. She did not give her heart to Jesus that first meeting, but she was drawn back. Then a few meetings later she surrendered her life to the Lord, and she soon joined the church. Not long afterward her husband began to come to church too. Eventually he met the Lord, and the marriage was saved.

This story illustrates the fact that woman-to-woman evangelism is very important in our church. We have more women than men, which is characteristic of most Christian churches, but that is not the reason we stress woman-to-woman evangelism. We have found that, when a woman becomes a Christian and is drawn into the fellowship of the church, her children will soon follow. This is almost a natural law. Where the women go for spiritual nourishment, they will take their children.

I realize that men are to be the spiritual leaders of their households, but men are not usually the first among the unbelievers to become interested in spiritual things. More often than not, the wife is the first one to be open to evangelism, and she is usually the first to commit her life to Jesus Christ. Frequently the husband is the last to come. He sees his wife and children going to church, and he sees they are getting something out of it. Usually he will go with them eventually, if only to find out what it's all about. If he then also can be drawn into a home cell meeting, we have found in our church that he will soon become caught up in the enthusiasm just as much as the rest of the family.

Today one of the greatest needs in the church is to evangelize our cities. It is not true that churches have to die in the central cities. I realize that materialism keeps many people away from the church and prevents them from opening their hearts and minds to the gospel. But our church is very successful in evangelism in the center of one of the world's largest cities. Seoul has more than eight million inhabitants. Yet in the past seven years we have gained 140,000 members, and we have also won thousands of others to the Lord and sent them to other churches. Our membership is now fifteen times larger than it was in 1973, when we moved to Yoido Island.

We have the same problems in trying to evangelize Seoul that any urban church has. There are many high-rise apartment buildings. It becomes difficult to meet new people in such circumstances. Christians just cannot go knocking on doors in an apartment building. (And besides, that is not our style of evangelism.)

However, one of our home cell leaders came up with a method. Every Saturday she began to spend a few hours riding up and down in the elevator of her apartment building. On many of those elevator rides she found opportunities to help people. One mother needed someone to carry her baby; an older woman needed help in carrying her groceries to the apartment. Always our cell leader was right there to offer help.

Little by little this enterprising leader became friends with many of the people she helped in the elevator. All the while she was secretly "planting" a home cell group meeting in her apartment building. While she was helping these people and making friends, she was silently praying for them. Eventually she obtained their telephone numbers from them, and she called them to invite them to a cell group meeting in her apartment.

She was so successful that today, if you go to any of the high-rise apartment buildings near our church on a

Saturday afternoon, you will find our cell leaders in the elevators, riding up and down, up and down. . . .

"Would you like me to help you carry your groceries?"

"Oh, please allow me to hold the door for you."

"Your faucet is leaking? My husband is very good at fixing faucets."

And so it goes; all the while seeds are being planted for home cell groups.

Our people are so enthusiastic about this kind of evangelism that even when they move away from Seoul they don't want to leave our church and our cell system. Four years ago one couple moved to Inchon, which is about twenty miles outside of Seoul. The wife was one of our cell leaders. When we talked, I said, "Well, I think you should join up with a good church in Inchon."

"Oh, no, Pastor Cho, that isn't what we want to do at all," the woman replied. "I think we will open our house for a cell meeting. Then on Sunday we will all get together and come to Seoul for church."

She had already begun to dream of the successful home cell group she would have in Inchon.

"Well, it's up to you," I said, and I gave her my blessing.

After that couple moved to Inchon, they did exactly as planned. Within a very short time they had a thriving home cell group, and on Sunday mornings they and their group would all come to church in a chartered bus! That was four years ago. Today that cell group has grown to 130 cells with 2,000 members in Inchon. Every Sunday they all charter buses to come to church.

One cell began to propagate and divide. Today Inchon is a full-fledged district of our church, with a licensed minister shepherding it.

That is quite remarkable. Without any evangelistic campaign, without any "revival meetings," without any fanfare, but with just the enthusiasm of a young Korean couple, we have 2,000 members in Inchon. In all that time I did not go once to Inchon to preach; the members all came to Seoul to hear me. These were 2,000 men, women, young people and children who met the Lord Jesus Christ through the zeal of that one couple.

Nowadays there are as many as 100 buses bringing members to our church every Sunday. Many visitors to Seoul look at that and say, "Oh, Yonggi Cho has a busing ministry. That must be the secret of his success. Look at how many buses he has!"

No, I do not charter a single bus. All of the home cell groups do this strictly on their own—to bring both members and newcomers to church. I have absolutely nothing to do with it. But I admit I'm happy it is taking place.

This is evangelism. This is church growth. By the end of 1980 we had 10,000 home cell groups. I firmly believe that when any church adopts this system of home cell groups, it is going to grow. If the church is already a large one, home cell groups are a real necessity for the members already in it; otherwise the pastor will have a nervous breakdown just trying to take care of the needs of his congregation, especially if he has more than 2,000 members.

In fact, I've been asked how many members I feel I could pastor successfully without a cell system. I don't think I could take care of more than 500. As it is now, I have to relate only to a relatively small number of leaders. Those leaders have others under them who shepherd the cell leaders, and it is the cell leaders who perform the bulk of the ministry in our church.

Full Gospel Central Church is not simply in the building that houses its offices and sanctuary; our church is out in the houses and apartment buildings, in the offices and factories of Seoul and its suburbs. The ministry is taking place out there. Evangelism is taking place out there. The central church building is the worship center where people come on Sundays and at other times to celebrate and worship, and to receive encouragement, education and edification.

Our church has become a living organism. The home cell groups are living cells, and they function much like the cells in the human body. In a living organism, the cells grow and divide. Where once there was one cell, there become two. Then there are four, then eight, then sixteen, and so forth. Cells are not simply added to the body; they are multiplied by geometric progression.

This is exactly what is happening with our home cell groups. When a home cell group reaches a membership of more than fifteen families, it divides into two. After that, the two new cells invite new people until they both exceed fifteen families again, and then they divide into four.

I already mentioned that in the beginning of our cell group ministry many people were reluctant to divide. Division had to be forced. That still happens occasionally, but most of the members of Full Gospel Central Church realize that the life of the group and of the church depends on constant cell division. Occasionally we have to send one of the pastors to persuade a cell group to divide, but generally the division takes place spontaneously when the group exceeds fifteen families. That is the rule in our church, and most of the members obey it without complaining.

Yes, there are often tears when friends have to separate to attend different meetings, but it is not a life-or-death situation. All of the cell groups are limited to specific geographical areas. If friends are no longer able to see one another in the cell meeting, they still get together at other times during the week, as all friends do, naturally. In addition, there are frequent district activities, where a number of cell groups get together for a picnic, a big prayer meeting or some other event.

There is one more thing that needs to be said about evangelism. The other side of evangelism is the back door of the church. Many churches complain that as many people are lost from the congregation through the back door as are won in revival meetings, and those churches are not growing. Well, there is practically no back door to our church. The reason is that each home cell group is like a family circle. Through these family circles people feel a sense of belonging, and they are kept in the church. On top of that, each cell leader watches over his or her little flock, just as a hen watches over her chicks. He is constantly caring for the needs of his flock. But at the same time, if one member of his cell group "plays hooky" from church, the following day the leader calls to find out if anything is wrong. If anything is, he can go and attend to it right away. Perhaps the person is ill or having some other problem that can be handled through prayer and ministry. And if he is really backsliding, the leader can determine the source of the problem and discuss it with him.

Therefore, once a person comes into our church through the cell system, we are not likely to lose him. Someone is always watching out for him, caring for him, helping him.

One day a man and his wife came into my office. They introduced themselves as new members of the church. Then the husband laughed, shook his head and said, "It is impossible to escape this church."

"What do you mean?" I asked.

The husband began to tell me the story of how his son had become a hippie. "We were very much worried about him," he said. "But then a very nice lady from this church came to our house. She was one of our neighbors. Well, she began to deal with my son. She talked with him and prayed with him, and after a while my son was completely changed.

"We really appreciated what she had done. She was so kind and nice.

"Then she invited us to come to her house for a visit, saying, 'We have a wonderful weekly meeting in our house. It is a wonderful time of fellowship, and we serve tea and cookies, and talk about religion. Would you come, please?'

"So out of appreciation we went. I must admit that we really did enjoy ourselves too. We listened to the singing, and the testimonies were very exciting. The message was good, and we even appreciated the concern of the people when they prayed for us and our son.

"But after the meeting was over, we didn't think too much more about it. We didn't think it was anything more than a nice evening with some of our neighbors.

"But then the next week this lady invited us again. So we thought it would be all right to go again, because we did enjoy ourselves the first time. But we never considered committing ourselves to anything on a regular basis.

"Then on Saturday she called us again and said, 'To-morrow is Sunday. Won't you come with me to our mother church? We have a wonderful pastor. He always has a good message. Let's go!'

"The next day she came in her car and honked the horn. So we went.

"I have to tell you in all honesty that we were shocked when we arrived at the church. We had never seen such a place! It was overwhelming, so big! But what really shocked us even more was how noisy it was. We had never seen people praying out loud like that before, and praising God and clapping their hands.

"After it was all over and we were home again, I said to my wife, 'Well, that was a fine church, I guess, but it was too noisy. I think some of those people were hysterical. I don't think we should go there any more.'"

They didn't realize it at the time, but they had already been hooked by our cell system. The next week the cell leader went over and invited them again to come to the meeting. After that she said, "I will pick you up again next Sunday for church."

"We tried to make excuses," the husband said, "but she very politely refused to accept them. So week after week we found ourselves going to the cell meetings and coming to church with the leader. Yet all the while we felt trapped and uncomfortable. We felt so harassed that we decided to sell the house and move!"

They called a real estate broker, sold their house and left the neighborhood, all without the knowledge of the cell leader. They took up residence in a distant part of the city, and the husband said to his wife, "At last we are free of that lady!"

So the next week when the leader went to invite them to the cell meeting, she found an empty house. But she was not ready to give up on them. She went down to the town hall and found their new address, wrote it down and brought it to the pastoral department of the church. There the clerks looked up the new address and turned it over to the cell leader for that area.

"I couldn't believe it," the husband told me. "There we were on Friday evening enjoying our freedom, when there came a knock on the door. I opened it, and there was this lady who said, 'Welcome to our area! I am the cell leader for Full Gospel Central Church, and you have been transferred to my section. Tonight we are coming to your house to celebrate!'

"So they came and held a service in our home. Again we sang and we prayed, and the group prayed for us in our new home. After it was over and everybody had left, I said to my wife, 'What are we going to do? To avoid this church we are either going to have to emigrate to America, or to heaven!'

"Then my wife said, 'Well, if we cannot avoid them, I guess the only thing to do is join them.'

"So the next Sunday we came to church, and we clapped and shouted just like everybody else. Now we have even become full members of the church."

Since then that couple has become an outstanding family in our congregation. It was all because of the persistence of the cell leaders. (I must add that it was all done in a very nice way, and the people were not in the least bit offended. In fact, I am convinced that all along they were under conviction by the Holy Spirit. They were not just trying to run from our church or our cell leader; they were really trying to run from God. When they found they could not escape Him, they surrendered.)

Not all of our leaders are so persistent, of course, and not all of them are as successful in persuading unbelievers to come to the meetings. But there is enough success that our church is really growing.

We need to let the sinners come to our churches and meet Jesus Christ; we need them to be saved. Then we should never let them leave. The only way a member should leave the church is either to transfer to a new church or to be buried in a casket.

In our church it is impossible for me to have personal contact with all 150,000 members. But through the cell leaders I do have contact in a secondary way with them. I am assured that our members are properly cared for, properly discipled, properly fed—and properly corrected when needed.

That is why we have real evangelism in our church! Our enthusiastic leaders are constantly bringing in unbelievers, and after they have them, they are meeting their needs so well that very few are lost out the back door.

7

A New Kind of Missionary

By now it should be evident that the cell system of Full Gospel Central Church is something that will work anywhere. In fact, it does! It is working both in other churches that have adopted this program and in missionary churches started by ministers from our own congregation, both in Korea and overseas.

Since Full Gospel Central Church began to be known for its rapid growth through the cell system, I have been called to speak at meetings and conferences all over the world. So many churches have been losing members. Or if they are not losing members, they are not growing. Everyone wants to know how to reverse the trend.

Several years ago I was invited to Australia by the Assemblies of God to discuss church growth. When I arrived, the denominational leaders who met me at the airport warned me not to expect too many people at the meetings.

"Australians are not churchgoers any longer," I was told. "They are worldly. Australia is rich with minerals, and many Australians have found material success without having to work very hard for it. Now they are much more interested in pleasures than in God."

What I saw around me on the ride from the airport confirmed what they were saying. Prosperity seemed to be all around me. In fact, it appeared that the Australians were living even better than the Americans. It was understandable that church officials did not have much faith that our growth principles would work, but they wanted to hear me anyway.

I knew I would really have to build some faith in those Australians when I arrived at the hotel where they were going to put me up. We had driven past the Sheraton and the Hilton hotels. When the car came to a stop, I could not believe my eyes. It was the YWCA! I soon discovered I was the only male guest there. When I entered the lobby, the girls all looked around at me, and I felt like an animal in the zoo. Later in the restaurant I was again the only man.

Immediately my heart went out to those church officials. Just to save a few dollars they had put me up in the YWCA. They had been preaching and praying, and putting on all kinds of evangelistic campaigns, but with no success. No wonder their faith was weak.

I went down to the kitchen to call my wife in Korea. She asked, "Where are you? How can I get in touch with you?"

"You cannot get in touch with me," I said. "I am in the kitchen of the YWCA, and I'm surrounded by girls on every side."

"Get out of that place right away and find yourself another hotel!" she exclaimed.

"I cannot move," I told her. "I don't want to hurt the feelings of the committee that brought me here."

From that first night I began to tell those church officials about faith and church growth. I especially stressed the need for setting goals, based on the experience of my own church, and I described our system of home cell groups.

"How can we possibly set goals such as those you are describing?" one of the ministers asked me. "For the past ten years we have had only 2 percent growth in the Assemblies of God throughout Australia."

Two percent, I thought. Why, that wasn't even growth; it was a decrease! The church was not even keeping pace with the rate of population growth, and so it now had fewer members in proportion to the size of the population than it had ten years earlier.

So I told them, "If you don't begin now to set goals and apply the principles of church growth, using the system of home cell groups, the Assemblies of God will die out in Australia."

I then asked every minister to set a goal before the end of the conference. I stressed the need to exercise faith principles. I told them to institute home cell groups.

I am happy to report that the ministers subscribed to my principles, and met with success. Within the next three years membership in the Assemblies of God increased 100 percent in Australia. They were amazed! In the preceding ten years they had grown only 2 percent using traditional forms of evangelism; but using our church growth principles they doubled in only three years. Now the Australian Assemblies of God are growing like wildfire.

Today I am concentrating 60 percent of my attention on Japan. Most churchmen and missionaries consider Japan dead. Japanese pastors are very discouraged. In fact, if a Japanese minister has thirty or forty members in his congregation, he can strut around like a big shot. Some pastors stick with twenty members throughout their whole lives. Understandably, once they are assured of a salary, many of them settle into a relaxed routine and give up the struggle to evangelize.

When I held a conference on church growth in Japan two years ago and told them the need to set goals, I was told, "There's no need to set goals here. This is Japan. You will find very few churches here that have more than 100 members. A church of 500 members is a great church in Japan."

They wouldn't listen to me. "Yes, churches are going to grow in Korea and America, and in Australia, but that is not possible in Japan."

Finally I was exasperated. I said to them, "I am going to prove that you are wrong."

It might be well to point out that in Japan the Korean people are despised. Our people had been under Japanese domination during World War II, until we were liberated by the Americans. We had been under Japanese occupation for thirty-six years. Therefore, the Japanese had come to consider themselves a superior people, while the Koreans were considered inferior.

Also in Japan, as elsewhere throughout the Orient, women are subservient to men, and they are actually treated as inferiors by men. Women especially have no place in ministry in Japan.

But I was so determined to prove my principles in Japan that I went back to Korea and selected one of the women staff members of our church to become a missionary to Japan. In fact, I selected a rather ordinary woman from among the licensed ministers, and I told her I was sending her to Japan. To my surprise, she told me she had already felt a calling to Japan!

So I said to her, "You know that the Japanese despise us Koreans. Besides that, you are a woman. You are going to have great difficulty. But I'm sending you right into downtown Tokyo, and I challenge you to start a church and make it grow to 1,000 members. I want you to reach that goal in five years. Use all the church growth principles you've learned.

"And if you don't accomplish your goal," I said, "don't come back to Korea."

Kamikaze, I thought.

That was two years ago. She went to Japan with a first-year goal of 200 members. She organized her first cell meeting and began to look for needy people. But most of the Japanese people just laughed at her. It was just as we thought. They took one look at her and said, "She is Korean, and besides that she is a woman! Who is going to listen to her?"

But we believed, and we prayed for her. Meanwhile, she fasted and prayed. Then at the end of her first year in Japan, I went over to visit her and to hold some meetings. What a joy it was to be welcomed into her new church! She had exceeded her goal, and she had 250 members—both Japanese and Koreans.

I had sent her to Japan with six months' salary. But when I arrived a year later, she presented me with an offering from her congregation of $2,000 to go toward the building fund of the mother church in Seoul. She had rented a 100-seat hall in an office building, and every Sunday she was holding three services. Toward the end of 1980 she was anticipating a membership of 500. I know she will have no trouble in reaching the goal of 1,000 members in five years.

When I was preaching in her church, I was delighted to see Japanese businessmen and ladies, all well-dressed and well-educated, flocking to church for the three services on Sunday. Their enthusiasm is fantastic!

Now when I go to Japan to attend the minister's conferences, I just stretch myself up as tall as I can, push my shoulders back and tell them, "Well now, this task of setting goals for churches in Japan, which you had considered so impossible, has been accomplished in just one year, and it has been done not only with a Korean, but with a woman. Here she is in downtown Tokyo, and she has 250 members! That is one of the largest Christian churches in the city! Shame on you!"

And they all dropped their heads, because they knew I was right.

So now in Japan many of the churches are beginning to catch fire just because of that one Korean missionary from our church. The Japanese men have to save face. Their reasoning is that, if a woman can do it and do it well, then the men should be able to do it better. That is Oriental thinking.

It should be obvious, then, that with the cell system I can send a missionary anywhere in the world, and he can start a church. All he has to do is begin looking for needs, loving people and helping them, and very soon he has the nucleus of a home cell group. As each cell grows and begins to divide, he soon has a church!

This has worked extremely well in Korea. In addition to our own church and its 10,000 home cell groups, fifty-five other churches have been started throughout the country by our members. They are now functioning as self-supporting churches within the Assemblies of God denomination, and they are all growing through home cell groups.

Our missionary churches are also springing up all over the world. There are now more than fifty churches started by our members outside of Korea, and more than forty of them are in North and South America. The largest has more than 500 members in New York City. We also have ten churches in Europe.

In most of these cases the churches were started to meet the needs of a local Korean community. Many Koreans have immigrated to the United States, Europe and South America. Some of them had been members of our church in Korea, or they had heard about it, or they had been to one of the other missionary churches that are part of the outreach of Full Gospel Central Church. They feel the need for churches in their own communities, and they ask us to send someone to lead them.

In each of these cases I have sent a missionary— always someone I have sent through Bible school and then trained as a licensed minister in our own church. I make sure they have at least three years of experience before I send them out. But when they are ready, and there is a call, I then provide them with a salary for six months to a year and let them start a church.

In every case the amount of money I have provided has been sufficient. After six months to a year every one of those missionary churches has become self-supporting. I do not have to keep sending them money endlessly, as some Western churches and denominations have done for their missionaries. The local congregations themselves provide everything necessary, including the missionary's salary.

8

The Miracle Church

I have explained that the growth of our church is based upon goal-setting and the establishment of home cell groups. I have more than realized the goals I have set so far. At the beginning of 1980 we had 100,000 members in Full Gospel Central Church. Now I have set 500,000 as my goal to be reached by 1984, the year in which we celebrate the 100th anniversary of Christianity in Korea.

When people heard I had set a goal of 500,000 for 1984, many asked me, "Are you going to have a big campaign? Are you going to have a city-wide soul-winning program?"

I don't need any of those things, because I have a completely different philosophy of evangelism. Before I knew the biblical way of evangelizing, I thought the only thing to do was have a big revival meeting with all sorts of special speakers and programs. But with the cell system, we don't need any special programs at all. We are having revival every day, and it hardly takes any effort.

To illustrate how revival is going on in our church, let me go back to June of 1980. At that time our congregation had reached 120,000. We had 8,000 cell groups. Only six months earlier we had set a goal of 30,000 new members in 1980. But in less than six months our 100,000-member congregation had grown to 120,000, two-thirds of our goal. So we increased the goal for 1980 to 150,000. I told each of the cell groups that they needed to lead only one family each to Christ for the rest of the year.

But with 8,000 cells, that would mean 8,000 more families by the end of the year. The average family size is about four persons. Therefore, adding 8,000 families to our church would actually bring in 32,000 new members during the remaining six months of 1980.

That's a great revival! And there's no fanfare, no need to push, no need to advertise. I simply motivate the cell leaders. Each cell group has only one family to lead to Christ. That's no problem. The ten to fifteen families in each cell group select one unbelieving family and begin to pray for them and witness to them. It's not difficult to understand that many of these cell groups will lead more than one family to Christ during that time; they will lead two or three.

So it is easy to see why we ended the year 1980 with 150,000 members and 10,000 home cell groups. Now I have increased the goal for 1981—to four families per cell. That will mean 80,000 new members in the first half of the year and 80,000 more in the second half. By the end of the year we will have 310,000 members. So it is easy to see how we can reach 500,000 members by 1984—with no problems, no fanfare, no television thrust, no mass distribution of tracts, just person-to-person contact through the home cell groups.

Because of the way this system works, there should be no plateaus to church growth. Too many churches grow to 500 or 1,000 members and then settle down and begin to mark time. It isn't that there are no more people to be won to Christ in their area; the minister simply becomes satisfied and loses the vision for evangelism. Then the work of the Holy Spirit begins to cool.

But with cell groups that evangelize, the church can continue to grow and thrive, no matter what circumstances it faces. Today we have an oil problem because of the situation in the Middle East. When any place is faced with a real oil shortage, and there is a lack of public transportation, church attendance will drop, unless the people live near the church building.

But that does not have to be a problem for our church. If the people cannot get transportation to come to church on Sundays, they will still receive ministry in the cell meeting, and they continue to be just as much a part of the church as if they were in the main church building every Sunday. For a larger meeting, groups of cells can get together for a district worship service in their own area, and the district pastor will do the preaching. There they will worship and take up offerings for the use of the mother church. If the oil shortage is a long one, I can make video cassettes of my message and have it shown to the district worship meetings.

In Korea, if there is ever a war in which the Communists take control of Seoul, one of the first things they will do is close the churches and kill the pastors. If I had built my church around myself, the church would be destroyed the moment I was removed from authority over it. But the way our church is set up, it is impossible to destroy it. When the Communists come and destroy the church building and kill me, all the church members will go underground. Yes, the Communists may be able to find and eliminate some of the cell groups, perhaps even hundreds of them. But they will never be able to find and destroy all 10,000 of them. The church will persist and remain underground.

The church in China has survived with just this kind of pattern. (I have a great deal of information on China because of my radio ministry.) In China there are only a few visible "legal" churches now, but those are really under the domination of the Communist government. The pastors cannot preach the full gospel in those churches.

But the church in China does not exist just in those few visible buildings. There are thousands and thousands of cell-group churches throughout the country. They are very similar to the cell groups in our church.

You can't meet the members of the cell groups casually, because they will not expose themselves to strangers. The only way to meet them is through an intermediary. But once you meet them, they will welcome you. I know of thousands of these Christian cells in the Canton area alone, and some of those cells constitute a fellowship of more than 500 persons.

When I first met members of those Chinese churches, on a visit to Hong Kong, the first thing they asked for was Bibles, and they wanted cassette tapes and recorders. Then they asked me, "Do the churches in the rest of the world have this full blessing of the Holy Spirit as we have in China?"

Most of the Chinese churches were started purely by the Holy Spirit. The people had never seen or heard a missionary, because the Communist Chinese government successfully removed Christianity as a part of public life during its more than thirty years in power. Yet most of the converts are under thirty-five years of age!

Another thing I learned about the cell-group churches in China is that 99 percent of the leaders are women. They took the leadership when the men were afraid to expose themselves as Christians.

The churches in China are thriving—without being under a mother church, without trained pastors or missionaries, without denominations. The life is being transmitted from cell to cell. Their experience demonstrates that the cell system is the answer for churches in these last days.

In an age of economic depression, how can a church carry out body ministry when it has such a large crowd of people as we have at Full Gospel Central Church? Again the answer is home cell groups. In the cell groups, members really care for one another. When someone is out of a job and has no income, other members of the group help to meet his needs. The care shown by the members of our cell groups is more than superficial affection. It is really love in action. Our people go out of their way, and even sacrifice, to meet the needs of a brother or a sister. It's just like the church of the apostolic age, where the members shared all of their material possessions.

When people see what is happening in our cell groups, when they see how the believers all have real love for one another, they are attracted to the groups. In those groups they find so much security that they never want to leave.

As I have already mentioned, this system of home cell groups does not depend on one person. In our church it does not depend on me. It depends on the ministry of the Holy Spirit, because He is the one who energizes the leaders. If I were to leave our church, I believe the church would lose no more than 3,000 members out of the total 150,000. Those members don't depend on me; they depend on one another and on the Holy Spirit.

Depression, oil shortages, persecution—none of these things need affect my church. It will continue to grow as long as the people adhere to the principles I've shown to them.

9

Authority With Love

When I started my church, it was only a little tent mission of the Assemblies of God in Korea. Today it is the largest single congregation of Christians in the world. We have grown to this size within the framework of the Assemblies of God denomination.

I say this to stress one point: The size, the strength and the influence of our congregation is not isolated from the overall Church of Jesus Christ, nor is it isolated from a denomination. We are in full fellowship with the Church universal and with our denomination. But first and foremost, we are a local church.

From the descriptions of our church, here and elsewhere, it would be easy for someone to wonder if I am forming my own denomination, or if my principles are acceptable to the larger church. I am happy to declare that there is no division or lack of acceptance in either case. I am demonstrating that the system of home cell groups works *within* the local church and *within* the established denominations.

In the past, many home groups have been established outside of the local church and outside of established denominations. Often they have come out of the charismatic renewal that has swept the churches in the past two decades. Christians who were newly baptized in the Holy Spirit found themselves misunderstood by their own churches. They sought fellowship and teaching in these groups, as well as in the Pentecostal churches.

Gradually some of those groups (although not the majority of them) began to conflict with the churches and to usurp authority from them. Members of the groups were "submitting" to the authority of the private group leaders rather than to their own pastors (who usually did not understand them). Thus the "discipleship" or "shepherding" controversy was born.

In some cases these independent groups led many Christians into bondage. No one could make a decision unless it was confirmed by the elders of the group. Personal communication with the Holy Spirit was discouraged as those in authority began to exercise greater control over the personal lives of the members, including telling them who they should marry and telling the younger members if they were permitted to have contact with their "unbelieving" parents.

Needless to say, some of those groups actually were transformed into minor cults. Innumerable lives were disrupted and relationships ruined. (I do not mean to imply that this is a logical progression to be expected from independent home groups. Most of them have provided a good form of fellowship for Christians who elected to remain in their own churches and who continued to submit willingly to the discipline of their own churches. And, of course, some of those independent groups grew into fine charismatic churches. The ones that went astray definitely were in the minority.)

I don't have the answer as to how one keeps a cult from developing in such circumstances. In fact, the Bible doesn't have an answer either, for it is evident that a number of them developed during the time of the apostle Paul. It depends on the leader and on the circumstances. The wrong combination can bring about catastrophe in the church. That is why it is so important for the leaders to be responsible to others in authority, such as to a denomination or to a fellowship of pastors outside their own local church.

My system of home cell groups and the Full Gospel Central Church developed within the Assemblies of God denomination. I am still responsible to the general superintendent in Korea. We have a good relationship; we don't always agree on everything, but we are part of a working, loving partnership that involves mutual respect. Our goal is unity. From time to time there have been some persons who have urged me to pull out of the Assemblies of God and become an independent church. They tell me I would have greater freedom to do anything I want without having to answer to anybody. But I never even gave those suggestions a second thought, because I believe in the need for unity. I believe we should always promote the unity of the body of Christ, and we should reject anything that seeks to divide the Church.

When a local church pulls out of its denomination, it is a bad model to display before the Church and before the world. It makes people wonder about Christianity, for they interpret such divisions as revealing a lack of the love that we preach.

All of these considerations keep me humble. I know I need my peers in the denominations. I need both their love and their loving correction. I need to be open with them, and my church and my financial records need to be open to their inspection. In that way nothing is done in secret to cause suspicions. In this way I feel secure in my own position.

Therefore, with the agreement of the elders and the denominational executives, home cell groups should work in any local church, in any denomination, if they follow the principles I am laying down in this book. Home cell groups must be integrated into the whole program of the local church, and their influence should not expand beyond the boundaries of the local church. We must make disciples of the members of our own church, not of the members of somebody else's church.

The discipleship program that grew out of the independent home groups actually became a form of sheep-stealing. No respectable pastor would advocate that. It's unethical. In fact, in our church when our members are looking for unbelievers to help and to invite to the home cell meetings, I tell them specifically to avoid those who already belong to other churches. We do not proselytize. (Of course, if someone voluntarily leaves his church to come to our church and our home cell meetings because his own church is not meeting his spiritual needs, that is another story. But we do not seek members from other churches.) In Korea the Christians often display a red cross on the doors of their homes to identify them as Christians. When our members see that symbol, they know the person behind the door is already a brother from another church, and they leave him alone.

The local church is the strength of Christianity. Home cell groups contribute to that strength. Anything that dilutes the strength of the local church is to be avoided. That includes some of the parachurch ministries that sometimes take money and commitment away from the local church. If a parachurch ministry or mission is contributing to the strength of the local church, it should be encouraged and supported. But if it weakens the local church, it should be discouraged and not supported. The local church is the preserver of faith and of Christianity.

I would also like to point out that, while there is a very tight structure in our church, the members have real freedom to be themselves. As I mentioned earlier, one of the problems with the independent home groups is that some of them have exercised too much control over their members. That is wrong. In our church the cell leaders are there to help oversee the spiritual growth of the members, and to encourage them in fellowship and evangelism. But they are never to meddle in the personal affairs of the members. That is not the responsibility of the church. Each member must be encouraged and taught to depend upon the Holy Spirit himself and to develop a life of faith. I never encourage our members to become dependent on the cell leaders, because that would be as bad as communism or the Moonies. Anything that destroys personal independence and the individual's personality and responsibility is from the devil. God never created us to be puppets. He gave us personalities to be developed into loving sons and daughters living in relationship with Him. Our home cell groups are designed to promote that relationship.

In our church we have "authority with love." If a pastor really loves the people in his congregation, they will respond to his authority and will obey his teaching. But if the pastor tries to exert his authority merely on the strength of his position or on human maneuvering, the people will rebel, and he will be in trouble.

The members of Full Gospel Central Church obey me because they know I genuinely love them. If I make a mistake, I publicly confess it to them and ask them to pray for me. When a pastor can be open with his congregation like that, they will respect him and obey him. In Christianity all authority must be based on love, just as God's authority over us is based on love.

Today many Christians do not respect their pastors or the authority of their pastors. That is wrong. The pastor has been anointed by God to lead the sheep, but he has to show real Christlike love to the sheep before they will follow him unreservedly.

I learned a lesson about taking church members for granted (thus showing a lack of love). Recently one of our elders told me that another elder had said, "I do not fully agree with all of Pastor Cho's policies in the church, but I accept them because I know he really loves me. He's doing all of this for our benefit."

I felt good about the man's allegiance, but I was disturbed that he had not told me what policies he disagreed with. When I finally approached him on the matter, he said, "You never consulted me when you appointed me head of the missions board for Europe. You knew I would do it, but you didn't ask me."

He was right. I had taken it for granted that he would accept.

"Please forgive me," I said to him. "I've taken your love and obedience for granted."

He responded immediately, and his confidence in me was multiplied that day. I developed a new respect for him as well, and the openness has contributed to an even better relationship between us. When people know that the pastor will admit his mistakes and will be honest with them, they will respect him.

10

Church Growth International

I have been telling people about these church growth principles since 1964, when I was invited to attend the General Council of the Assemblies of God in Springfield, Missouri. In fact, that was the year I really began to travel, in spite of my illness and weakness at that time. Between 1964 and 1973 I was out of Korea at least three times a year, mainly to Japan, the Philippines and Taiwan, to talk about home cell groups and church growth.

After we moved to Yoido Island in 1973, our church began to become better known. That was the year Billy Graham held his big crusade in Seoul, and it also was the year the World Pentecostal Conference met in our church. In addition, the following year Campus Crusade for Christ sponsored a big conference in Seoul.

With so many Christian events occurring in Seoul, our church was becoming increasingly an international attraction. Invitations began to pour in, asking me to travel to America, to Europe, to Australia and to Southeast Asia to discuss church growth.

Beginning in 1973 I found myself traveling outside of Korea for up to six months a year. Surprisingly, most of the invitations were coming from Europe. I was invited to speak in West Germany, France, Switzerland, Norway, Denmark, Sweden, England, Italy and Portugal. My books, which I continued to write, were becoming best sellers in Germany, Sweden and Finland. I was better known in Europe than in America.

On one of those trips in 1976 I had just completed a series of meetings in Germany. The seminars had been very well attended. On the Lufthansa flight leaving Germany, I was praying in my seat, thanking God for the wonderful time of sharing, and really feeling close fellowship with the Holy Spirit.

Suddenly a very strong sensation of prophecy came upon my heart, as the Holy Spirit said to me, *"When you get back home, I want you to build an international church growth training center to which you can invite pastors from all over the world. You are doing a good work in carrying this message throughout the world with your seminars, but I want to multiply the number of pastors who will learn these principles. The best way is for them to see firsthand what you are doing right in Seoul. Build a training center. Let them come and learn from you and see your church in operation.*

That is the best way for them to gain the enthusiasm they need to put this dimension of evangelism into their own ministries."

I was shocked. "How can this be, Lord?" I asked. "I am from a Third World country. We are what is called the 'mission field' by Western Christians. Surely such a training center ought to be built in the United States or Europe."

But the thought would not go away. I wondered about it all the way back to Korea. Afterward, when the thought persisted at home, I decided to spread a fleece.

"Lord, if this desire in my heart is from you, then I ask you to show me," I said. "If the people of our church will contribute enough money in one offering to build a missions center, that will be the sign that I should proceed."

I discussed the proposal with the elders, and we decided to schedule a Sunday when we would ask the members to give one million dollars (either in cash or in pledges) for the construction of the missions center. To tell the truth, it was more than I could believe for at that time. I was really worried and afraid that the people would not give.

Finally I just said in my prayer, "Father, if this is your will, give me the one million dollars. If I do not receive it on Sunday, I will forget the whole thing."

The next Sunday the offerings and pledges came in. When they were all tallied up, the finance chairman brought me the final figures: exactly one million dollars!

Immediately we set the process in motion to construct the World Mission Center right next to Full Gospel Central Church, and we formed a new organization to carry out this portion of my ministry: Church Growth International.

As the plans began to take shape, I knew this was a major undertaking. I also knew I would not be able to handle it alone. I still had our church to lead, and the demands of Church Growth International also called for a full-time executive. I could not do both jobs. Who would I get to lead it?

Then the name of John Hurston suddenly came to mind: the missionary who had worked with me in my little tent church in the poor area of Seoul, the missionary who had played such a major role in founding the West Gate church with me. I had not seen him in more than five years. John Hurston had been with me for ten years until he left in 1969 to go to Vietnam. There he started several churches during the Vietnam War. He finally had to flee in 1975 when the Communists took over South Vietnam.

I traced John to Pasadena, California, where I found him recuperating from a minor heart attack. When I visited him, he looked very tired, and he appeared much older than when I last had seen him five years earlier.

"It was a very traumatic experience to leave Vietnam," he admitted. "I spent six years there building churches, and I literally wept when I had to leave them as I did.

But I knew I had no choice."

"John, what are you planning to do now?" I asked.

"I don't know yet," he said. "The Missions Board has asked me to go to Thailand, to be director of missions for the Assemblies of God there. But frankly I don't feel any leading at all in the matter."

That was the opening I needed. I began to explain the vision God had given me for building Church Growth International, and I told John how He had provided the money to build it.

"I need an executive director," I said. "I believe you are the man for the job, John."

I could see immediately that the idea appealed to him, and so we prayed about it.

"Yes, I think that is the job the Lord would want me to take," he said at last. "But if I am to take over such a responsible job now, God will have to heal me of this heart condition."

The following month my mother-in-law, Dr. Jashil Choi, was holding some meetings in the Los Angeles area. At that meeting she laid hands on John, and he felt a definite healing. Not long after that he was on his way back to Korea.

There was one other thing I felt the Lord wanted me to do in giving Church Growth International a firm foundation. We needed an international advisory board to give us their input on how we could make the resources of our facility available to the most ministers. Shortly after the World Mission Center was finished in

November, 1976, I began to look for those advisors.

The following February I set up a meeting in a hotel in North Hollywood, to which I had invited two dozen ministers from thriving churches in America. I was amazed when almost all of them showed up.

At that first meeting I described the vision the Lord had given me for spreading church growth principles around the world by means of the new organization.

"I specifically feel we are to share our knowledge with the churches in Third World countries," I said. "In that way we will be strengthening the church in those countries and encouraging them to greater growth for worldwide evangelism."

Everyone was very enthusiastic about the vision. I suggested that one of them be nominated as chairman of our group.

"Oh, no, no, you are the one who has the vision for church growth," I was told. "We came here because of you. We wouldn't have come otherwise."

So they unanimously elected me chairman and agreed to work together with me in setting up Church Growth International meetings, not only in Korea but also in the United States and elsewhere around the world.

I really feel that Church Growth International is addressing the needs of the church in the 1980s. This is going to be the era of church growth. The 1960s were an era of healings that helped to spread the renewal of the churches. The 1970s were the era of the charismatic movement. Now it's time for church growth. Healings and charismatic renewal will do no good for the church unless they contribute to the growth of the church. In fact, all the gifts of the Holy Spirit are given to build up the body of Christ, and that does not mean only spiritual encouragement; it includes physical growth as well.

We must be serious about church growth if we are concerned about the future of the Church of Jesus Christ. Church growth is not just another fad. Jesus came to build a Church, and that Church has been asleep until now. It is just waking up! Any church that wakes up is going to grow.

The kind of growth we are experiencing in Korea is available to all of the churches. I know there are some who think this is only a Korean phenomenon that does not apply to the United States or to Western Europe. But these are solid, proven principles of church growth that have merely been demonstrated in our church in Korea. There is no reason why any other church could not grow to the same size—or larger—using these principles. They are universal, as applicable in Seattle, or Sydney, or Stockholm, as they are in Seoul.

We are all children of Adam. We eat different kinds of food, but we all have the same kind of blood. We are all sinners in need of salvation by Jesus Christ. We all need to be empowered by the Holy Spirit. If a church preaches the gospel, the Word of God, with the power of the Holy Spirit, it is going to grow. Then, if it adds these principles of church growth and establishes home cell groups, it is going to be a strong and *rapidly* growing church.

These principles *will* work—anywhere in the world. To think otherwise is dangerous, for that would mean believing that God works one way in one place and another way someplace else. He is powerful in Korea but not so powerful elsewhere. That cannot be true. A principle is always a principle. If a church adopts these principles, if it starts home cell groups, it will find everything following the same pattern that we have in our church, and it will grow.

This teaching has really revolutionized the churches of Australia. I've already mentioned that the Australian Assemblies of God had experienced only 2 percent growth in ten years before they adopted my principles; afterward they doubled in only three years. I might also add that there are now two Assemblies of God churches in that country with more than 2,000 members each, one in Adelaide and one in Brisbane. Until they adopted my church growth principles, the Australian churches were much like those in Japan—forty or fifty members was the usual size of the congregation.

There was one Lutheran church in Europe that had only fifteen people in church each Sunday. Then the pastor attended one of my seminars and put my church growth principles into practice. Within one year of forming his first cell groups, his church continually increased in attendance until now he has 500 people in church every Sunday. In addition, that church soon learned there was something missing in their experience, and they discovered the power of the Holy Spirit. Their cell groups really sprang to life, and the church is now fully charismatic.

I am now concentrating my efforts on Japan. The missionary in Tokyo with her growing church (soon to be 500 members) is only the beginning. We are believing the Holy Spirit can bring ten million Japanese to Christ in the 1980s, and we are working with Him to bring those people into the church by using our church growth principles.

Church Growth International has really proven itself to be a sovereign move of the Holy Spirit. The fruit it has borne is evidence of that.

11

How to Begin Home Cell Groups

There is only one way that the home cell group system will be successful in a church, if that system is to be used as a tool of evangelism. The pastor must be the key person involved. Without the pastor, the system will not hold together. It *is* a system, and a system must have a control point. The controlling factor in home cell groups is the pastor.

So if you are a layman reading this book, the first thing I would recommend is that you give a copy of the book to your pastor. Then pray that he will read it and catch the vision. You cannot start anything without him. When he reads the book, sees the potential for church growth and becomes motivated to start something himself, he will be in a good position to inaugurate home cell groups. After he has had a chance to digest the contents of the book, call him up and invite him to breakfast or lunch. Then you can discuss home cell groups as a means of church revival and evangelism.

From that point on, it is up to the pastor to motivate the congregation toward revival and toward church growth using the principles of home cell groups. It is up to you to support him and work with him in getting the congregation involved.

If your church can afford it, I would recommend sending the pastor to one of our Church Growth International seminars. They are being held all over the world, and we will be happy to provide you with a schedule. The best seminar is the one in Seoul, where one can see firsthand what has been accomplished at Full Gospel Central Church.

I know of many churches that have attempted to set up home cell groups without the central involvement of the pastor. They have all struggled without any real success. There is one big church in the United States whose pastor attended our seminar in Seoul and saw the value of cell groups. But instead of getting behind the effort and promoting cell groups himself, he turned all of the responsibilities over to an associate minister. The associate did all of the organizing, and the cell groups were started. But after two years they are stagnant; attendance is poor and the members are not being motivated toward evangelism. Why? The congregation sees cell groups as only one of many varied programs in this big church. They don't see them as the key to revival or to evangelism; after all, there are so many other programs aimed at those goals. The pastor isn't actively involved, so the members feel that cell groups can't be all that important.

If cell groups are to succeed, the pastor must become so convinced of their necessity in the church that he will see them as the key to the life or death of his church. Once he becomes convinced, the program will move.

A lot of groundwork needs to be laid before the system can be implemented. I believe the pastor needs to commit his energy and leadership to lay the groundwork. And even after the program is rolling, he needs to remain the obvious leader, training the cell leaders and motivating them to reach the goals that have been established for each group.

The nitty-gritty can be delegated to an associate, but the leadership must remain with the pastor. He must continue to have an active relationship with the cell leaders.

I always say that a minister should put his total energy into this system to make it successful. That calls for a concentration of power and enthusiasm. Otherwise the people will feel that the system of home cell groups is only a gimmick, and the church today has become very callous about gimmicks. Any gimmick is bound to fail, but cell groups are not a gimmick.

If the people are not convinced the pastor is behind the formation of cell groups, one of three things will occur:

1. The system will bog down and begin to stagnate.

Cells will meet for "fellowship" only, and there will be no real spiritual growth and no evangelism. Eventually they will fizzle out.

2. Meetings will become ritualistic, or the groups will come under the influence of personalities. In this way the cells eventually will become something superfluous, useless and harmful.

3. The system will become a cancer on the local body if the cell leaders are not required to report regularly to their peers or superiors, or to the pastor.

Even in Korea many churches that have organized cell groups as a result of seeing the success of our church have found the system of no use to them because the pastor is not the central figure in it. Some of them think that just because I am traveling six months out of the year I cannot possibly be giving personal direction to the cell groups. But I really do. When I am traveling, I always record my messages for the cell leaders on video cassettes. The fellowship leaders need to feel they are a top priority of the church so they are motivated to work and take responsibility. If I don't give them that personal attention, they are not so motivated.

The pastor who decides to become involved in home cell groups needs to study this system thoroughly, or he will fail. And if he fails once, he will not be inclined to try it again. It is very important for him to attend a church where the cell system is operating successfully. Once he understands it clearly, then it is time for him to begin.

The first steps in establishing home cell groups are very important. Here are my recommendations for the pastor:

First, you should start small. Take a dozen key lay leaders and train them as cell leaders. Then have them form their own home cell meetings, and watch over them carefully for six to eight months. Once this group of cells has begun to bear fruit, it will be time to get the whole church involved.

Selecting the right lay leaders is essential. Success or failure can depend on them. The first thing the pastor should do is look for men and women who are Spirit-filled. If the leaders are not dependent on the Holy Spirit, they can actually begin to move counter to the work of the Holy Spirit. Here are some of the qualities I look for in cell leaders:

1. *Enthusiasm.* New Christians often make very good cell leaders, because they have just come into a personal relationship with Jesus Christ. Their enthusiasm is infectious. Older Christians often need to be reprogrammed before they will accept the cell system.

2. *Testimony.* Christians who have a clear, powerful testimony of what God has done for them are living proofs that the gospel does work today. Such Christians demonstrate the reality of the life of Christ, and others are drawn to them.

3. *Dedication.* You can usually tell whether a person is dedicated to the Lord and to your church by (a) his attendance record at church and at other meetings,

including cell groups, (b) his tithing record, which is an essential part of his life of faith, and (c) his demonstrated commitment to unity in the life of the church. Those who are overcritical or out of step with the majority will not easily follow the pastor's directions for leading home cell groups.

4. *Spirit-filled.* Dependence upon the Holy Spirit is essential if a person is to lead the members of his cell group. In our church that means the leader must be baptized in the Holy Spirit, with the evidence of speaking in tongues. Then we are assured of a person who can lead others to Christ and who can pray powerfully for the people's needs. This is particularly essential in praying for physical and spiritual healing.

5. *Time and money.* Although there is an axiom that, if you want a job done, give it to a busy person, that axiom does not apply to spiritual leadership. The busier a person is, the less time he is going to have to listen to and receive direction from the Holy Spirit. The best cell leaders are those who do not have to go to work outside the home; they usually have much more time for prayer and Bible study. The same holds true for those with enough money that they don't have to be concerned constantly about earning enough to live on; they too will have more time for prayer and Bible study. This does not mean we should not select poor people to lead home cell groups, however. If people meet all of the other qualifications, I am convinced they will make good cell leaders. And besides, they probably will not

remain poor for long. I teach our people that when you go to work for the Lord you are not going to stay poor, because God is going to supply all your needs.

Once the leaders are selected, they need to be trained in leading meetings. First they must learn from the pastor so that they can pass on the pastor's teaching to those in the cell groups. It is essential that the teaching at cell meetings fit in with the overall program of teaching in the church. It is a good idea for cell group lessons to follow the pastor's Sunday sermon, perhaps to enlarge upon some of the most important points of that sermon.

I provide all of my cell leaders with a standard lesson each week. In an earlier chapter I mentioned the chaos that resulted from a lack of direction in the early days of cell groups in our church. That settled down when I began to write out the lesson plan for all of the cell meetings each week. I no longer have time to prepare individual lesson plans each week, but our church has adopted a standard Bible study course for cell groups similar to the standard Sunday school courses available in many churches.

Although I no longer prepare the individual lessons, I still take an active role in preparing the leaders. At first the leaders all met with me each Wednesday evening in place of the midweek prayer meeting to learn the next week's lesson. Later, when I could not be with them in person, I taught them via cassette tape. Now that our church has enlarged facilities, I teach them each week via video cassette. And each week the lesson outline appears in our church's weekly newspaper, so all of the members can prepare for the lesson in advance.

In addition to the lessons from the Word of God, there are other functions of a cell meeting that make it truly a gathering of God's people. There is always worship, through the singing of hymns and choruses, and through the prayers of the leader and others in the group. We always give the groups a time of open prayer, when all are permitted to bring their prayers of thanksgiving, confession, intercession and petition before the Lord.

A third ingredient of our cell meetings is ministry to one another. Members are encouraged to share their prayer needs so all can pray for them. We have had some miraculous healings take place right in the cell groups, as one person has prayed for another, making it clear to everyone that the Holy Spirit works in those meetings just as He does in the church services.

And finally, the meetings are required to be evangelistic. The lesson and the testimonies should lead newcomers to the person of Jesus Christ. Members are encouraged to look around their neighborhoods for unbelievers they can invite to the meetings. Many of those unbelievers do meet Jesus Christ and commit their lives to Him right in the cell meetings. This is really what is causing our church to grow so rapidly. To me, evangelism is essential if home cell groups are to provide real life for the church.

After the original group of cells has been meeting for six to eight months, it is time to expand to the whole congregation. By then the first cells should be bearing real fruit for the church, and most of the people will already have learned a great deal about them through the church grapevine. Now is the time to have an all-church meeting and introduce everybody to them.

At the general church meeting, the cell leaders and members of their groups should give testimony to the whole congregation, showing what God is doing through the cell meetings. Believe me, it will be an exciting time. The enthusiasm of the leaders and cell members will be infectious. People will be convinced that the cell system has something for them.

You should also have statistics to back up the testimonies, showing how many people have been healed or helped in other ways at the meetings, how many unbelievers have been led to Christ, and so on.

Each pastor should know his own church and how to get the most members involved. In our church I was able to assign everybody to a cell group. Although there was some initial grumbling, everybody went. That is the pattern in our church. However, other pastors tell me that voluntary participation is the only thing that will work in their churches. They distribute sign-up sheets at the all-church meeting, and the number of people who sign up determines the number and location of the cell groups. Whichever way the church goes, all efforts should be made to get the maximum participation.

For instance, there is one church in the United States that got involved in cell groups without using our model at all. The pastor was convinced our system would not work there. So he decided just to hold home meetings once a month, strictly for fellowship.

Although he started out differently, he did follow one of my principles: He directed the groups himself, and he appointed six or seven pastors under him to be a model cell group and use their experience to lead other groups. He did not believe it was necessary to divide the church up geographically, because everything was strictly voluntary.

Do you know what happened? Everybody who went to the home meetings enjoyed them so much that attendance grew quickly. Soon they had to meet more frequently. Not only that, but prayer and Bible study soon became a regular part of the format. It just happened naturally.

Now every new member of that church is required to sign up for a cell group, and they are encouraging the remaining older members to sign up too. The groups have become a major tool of evangelism, and the pastor now says it is almost as though a whole new church is growing within the original congregation—a church within a church—and the new inner church is livelier than the original one.

In California, another pastor already had a growing

church, and he was having difficulty fitting all of the people into his church building on Sundays for four or five services. So he divided his congregation into four groups. Each Sunday one of those groups would meet in various homes for fellowship and teaching, while the three other groups would meet at the main building for the regular Sunday worship services. Each of the groups would alternate at holding home meetings on Sundays, so that only three-fourths of the congregation attended formal worship each week. When there was a fifth Sunday in the month, everybody would come together at the church for a big celebration.

Again the pastor was in firm control of the home meetings. He trained the leadership and met with them weekly. He directed them in the Bible studies, which went along with what the pastor was teaching each week, and he gave the leaders an outline and a tape.

In addition to meeting once a month for Bible study, the groups in that church meet together one extra weekday during the month just for fellowship. Each group of cells has a picnic or some other form of social activity.

In these ways two pastors have found a way to bring home cell groups successfully to their churches without throwing their congregations into an uproar. Many American churchgoers complain of having to spend too much time in church, but by breaking their congregations into home cell groups those pastors have increased church attendance without making it seem like "church."

In Korea, however, our church does not have home meetings that are strictly for fellowship. It is all right for our members to meet for fellowship on their own, but I believe the meetings need to be highly disciplined if they are to produce the kind of evangelism and growth we have seen at Full Gospel Central Church. Groups that meet without having evangelism as a goal do not produce growth in the church. There is a great danger that they will only feed on themselves.

I think I should add one thing about the church I left behind in the West Gate area of Seoul. When we moved to Yoido Island, 8,000 of our members stayed behind at the old church, while 10,000 moved to the new one. The members who stayed behind got a new pastor, and they continue today to be a strong Assemblies of God church. But the new pastor did not adopt my principles of home cell groups. Although there are cell meetings in that church, they are not used as a tool of evangelism. The congregation, meanwhile, has dwindled to 2,000 members. (Many of the original 8,000 transferred to our church, although we had not sought them.)

I do not believe the traditional pastoral structure is capable of ministering to the needs of 8,000 members. Delegation of authority and the formation of home cell groups is the only way of meeting all of those needs.

12

Importance of Fellowship
With the Holy Spirit

I have already given the basic requirements for home cell group leaders in the preceding chapter. But I would like to elaborate on one of the points, namely the need for each leader to be filled with the Holy Spirit and guided by the Holy Spirit. In fact, the need goes beyond being filled and being guided—each leader must have real *fellowship* with the Holy Spirit.

Such fellowship with the Holy Spirit needs to be prompted by the pastor, who should already be having fellowship with the Holy Spirit. If the pastor is not experiencing fellowship with the Holy Spirit, he will not be able to help his cell leaders to grow in their own relationship with the Holy Spirit.

I would also like to illustrate this point from my own life. I give the greatest importance to fellowship with the Holy Spirit. I know that in my own preaching ministry, if I don't have the anointing of the Spirit, my message will not bring results, no matter how much time I spend in the preparation of my sermon. And if the message does not bring results, it is wasted.

Many people do not know the meaning of fellowship with the Holy Spirit. They say they are born again and have received the baptism in the Holy Spirit. They have experienced the power of the Holy Spirit in ministry.

"So what more do we need?" they ask.

That's a great mistake. I lived with that attitude myself for quite some time. I felt I had all the diplomas needed to be a preacher in my denomination. I was born again, I had received the baptism in the Holy Spirit, and I had spoken in tongues. "So that's all I need," I said to myself.

But God changed my attitude and showed me that the Holy Spirit is more than the Spirit of being born again, more than the Spirit of power. He's a person— but a person who lives inside me. To live with a person means to have fellowship with that person. It means recognition of each other. It means *intimate* fellowship and communication.

Before I discovered this truth, my ministry fluctuated greatly. Sometimes I would preach a very good message and have tremendous results. At other times my ministry seemed to flounder. Every Sunday when I really "hit a home run" with my sermons, I would come home rejoicing. At other times I seemed to strike out. I didn't see anybody being saved, and I would feel very depressed. I cried to the Lord and asked why He wasn't helping me.

Then one cold winter day in 1960, after preaching at the early morning prayer meeting, I was praying alone in the church when God began speaking to my spirit.

"My son," He said, *"if you could have a deeper fellowship with the Holy Spirit, your ministry would be multiplied and empowered greatly."*

So I said, "Father, don't I already have all of the Holy Spirit? I'm born again. I've been baptized in the Holy Spirit. What more do I need?"

Then God said, *"Yes, you have the Holy Spirit in a legalistic way, but you don't have intimate fellowship with the Holy Spirit. You may bring a wife into your home legally, but you may also leave her alone in the home as a thing, not as a person, if you don't have fellowship with her continually."*

That revelation brought new mileage to my ministry. I began to have real fellowship with the Holy Spirit.

I realized that in the past my fellowship had been similar to what is recorded in 1 John 1:3, which says, "Our fellowship is with the Father and with his Son, Jesus Christ" (NIV). Like most Christians, I had what I felt was fellowship with the Father and with His Son. I prayed to the Father, and I prayed to the Son, Jesus Christ. I worshiped the Father and I worshiped the Son. And like most Christians, I mentioned the Father and I mentioned the Son, but very seldom did I mention the Holy Spirit.

But when we read the Bible, it not only commands us to have fellowship with the Father and with His Son, Jesus Christ, it also commands us to have fellowship, or *communion,* with the Holy Spirit (2 Cor. 13:14).

The meaning should be clear. The Father finished His work in Old Testament times. Then He sent His Son, Jesus Christ, who was crucified and resurrected. Now, seated on the right hand of God the Father, Jesus has finished His work. Today we have the age of the Holy Spirit. The Father is working through the Holy Spirit, and Jesus is working through the Holy Spirit. So the Holy Spirit is the administrator of the love of God and the grace of Jesus Christ.

Communion in the Greek language is *koinonia,* which has several meanings: (1) fellowship, (2) partnership and (3) distribution. The love of God and the grace of Jesus Christ are constant, but they are in heaven. How then are they brought to our hearts right now in this hour here on earth? It is through the communion of the Holy Spirit.

So if we have a lot of theological knowledge about the love of God and the grace of Jesus Christ but don't have the communion of the Holy Spirit, there will be no reality of them in our hearts. There will be no distribution of the Father's real love and the Son's real grace into our hearts. We may have all of the theology and yet have an icebox in our church.

So a preacher may bring a tremendous message, with wonderful theology and very profound truth from the

Bible, but if he doesn't have definite cooperation from the Holy Spirit, it will be only theory. He is not preaching from his experience of the love of God and the grace of Jesus Christ. That is the main problem with the church throughout the world today. We have beautiful buildings, wonderful choirs, well-educated ministers and brilliant messages, while the people in the pews are starving to death. They have all sorts of knowledge poured into their minds, but their spirits are arid and starved.

Koinonia also means partnership. In a business partnership one person brings the finances and another brings the technology. Together they make the business successful. We are in the King's business. The Holy Spirit brings all the finances: the love of God and the grace of Jesus Christ. We bring our physical presence. So the Holy Spirit asks us to have a partnership with Him in building the Kingdom of God. The Holy Spirit is the Senior Partner, and we are the junior partners. The trouble nowadays is that the junior partners are trying to overrule the Senior Partner by doing the work on their own. Therefore, the Senior Partner pulls out, leaving the junior partners with good buildings (really, a good shopping center) but no commodities.

To be successful in the King's business, there needs to be a very, very close partnership with the Holy Spirit, and to do this there must be fellowship.

When we have fellowship with the Father, we address Him and say, "Father, I love you, I recognize you.

Praise God!" And to the Son we say, "Jesus, I love you, I praise you." But when we come to the Holy Spirit, what do we do? Often we do nothing.

The Bible commands us to have *communion* with the Holy Spirit, which includes all of those other three: fellowship, partnership and distribution. Without communion with the Holy Spirit, you can't have effective fellowship with the Father and with His Son, Jesus Christ.

Nowadays I always force myself to recognize the Holy Spirit, to welcome the Holy Spirit and to worship the Holy Spirit, because He is a person. Every time before I go out to preach, I always say, "Dear Holy Spirit, I welcome you, I recognize you and I love you. I depend upon you. Dear Holy Spirit, let's go! Let's bring the glory of God to the people!"

When I start to preach, I say in my heart, "Dear Holy Spirit, now I'm starting. Let's go! Supply all the knowledge and wisdom and discernment, and I'm going to give it out to the people."

After finishing the sermon, I will sit down and say, "Dear Holy Spirit, we did a wonderful job together, didn't we? Praise God!"

Since I have come to depend on the Holy Spirit in this way, I have felt a mighty anointing of God on my life and in my ministry and sermons. Always there are tremendous results and numerous conversions as well as healings. I try to float on the wave of the Holy Spirit.

To illustrate this in another way, I'll relate a story.

Once I almost lost my wife. When I got married, I was very much interested in becoming a famous evangelist. I wanted to be sort of a Korean Billy Graham. I didn't really want to be "just a pastor" in those days.

So after my wife and I were married, I brought her to our apartment, and after about a week I began to go out on evangelistic preaching missions. I would preach in my church on Sunday, and then on Monday I would go out preaching. I came home only on weekends and brought my laundry to my wife. This went on for six months while I burned with ambition to become an evangelist.

For a while my wife was very kind. When I came back from my evangelistic campaigns, she would rush out to the door and welcome me. She loved me, and she would cook a good meal for me. But as month after month passed and there was no change in this routine, she began to become depressed. She wouldn't welcome me. She cried often. Even the meals were not very good. Something was wrong.

At that time my wife was very shy, because we were only newly married. She never said anything to me about what was wrong. I tried to cheer her up by joking and so on, but nothing seemed to help.

Finally one day my mother-in-law came to me and said, "Yonggi, do you like living with my daughter?"

"Yes, of course," I said.

"Well," she said, "you are going to lose her if you keep treating her this way."

"Why, what do you mean?" I asked, shocked. "I treat her very nicely. I got her this nice apartment, and I make sure she has plenty of food and very good clothes. What more can I do? I'm treating her very nicely."

Then my mother-in-law looked into my eyes and said, "Son, you don't understand. You didn't bring a 'thing' into your home. You brought a *person* to your home. A person can't live in an apartment with just rice and clothes and money. She needs love, recognition, fellowship."

I thought about that for a long time. My immediate reaction was, "That's from the devil! Here I am working for the Lord. Why should she put so many demands on me for affection, care and concern?"

But my wife continued to become more and more depressed, and eventually some warning signs stirred in my heart. So I went before the Lord, and I prayed, "Lord, it seems that I am going to have to choose between one of two things—my ministry or my wife. Your glory and my ministry are far more important than my wife. If I need to lose one of them, then I will have to lose my wife, because my ministry means more to me than she does.

"God, either correct her or let us be separated. I'd rather live the rest of my life alone and carry on my ministry."

Then the Holy Spirit spoke to my heart, and He said, *"No, no, no. You are greatly mistaken in your priorities. So far you have put God first, church second, yourself third, and you are putting your wife last. You have made a grave mistake.*

"Of course, God must be first, but the rest of your priorities need to be rearranged. You should come second, and your wife should come third. When you have children, they should come fourth, and then the church should be last."

I thought about that, and I was in great consternation. "This must be an American devil!" I said. "We can't accept this kind of thinking in the Orient."

"Oh, no, this is not from America," the Holy Spirit said. *"This is my way.*

"God must be first, but you must come second, because you need to live a holy life to carry out this ministry. You are very important.

"Next, your wife must come right after you. If you ever lose your wife and become divorced, no one will ever listen to you again. Your ministry will be gone. You may build a tremendous church, but if your home becomes broken, you will lose your ministry. Having fellowship with your wife is more important than building a church, because the whole church is dependent on your home life. You will bring more disgrace to the ministry by being divorced than all the other benefits you might otherwise bring.

"Also, all the Christians will be looking at your children. If your children become rebellious and get into trouble, like the prodigal son, who is going to listen to you? Your primary ministry should be to your children.

Your children should be the number-one members of your church. Then all together, you, your wife and your children will build the church.

"Take your wife as a very important asset to your ministry, and nurture your relationship with her."

I thought that sounded quite risky at the time, but I decided to give it a try. I canceled a lot of my evangelistic campaigns, and I made a definite promise to spend every Monday with my wife. I said I would do anything on Mondays that my wife wanted me to do. If she wanted to go to the park, I would go with her to the park. If she wanted to go to the department store, I would almost break my backbone in following her, but I would do it. Then we would sit down and have a nice dinner together.

And every morning I would say to my wife, "Honey, I love you. You are very pretty. You're wonderful. I'm a lucky guy to have you."

Then a miracle occurred. My wife began to pull out of her depression. Her expression changed, and that buoyant spirit returned to her heart. She began to smile, and then to laugh and be cheerful and mischievous. After a while she began to cook good meals again. We had wonderful fellowship!

We began to pray together and to plan the ministry together. I had found the answer. To have a real home life you need to have real fellowship with each person. You can't bring your wife home and expect her to live there alone with only the house, the money, the clothes and the food. A wife is more than that; she's a person.

That is just what it's like to have fellowship with the Holy Spirit. The Holy Spirit is there with you, but if you just leave Him alone in the corner of your church, just using Him as a decoration in pronouncing the benediction or a word of theology, the Holy Spirit will become grieved. Then the Spirit of the Lord will leave your work, and you'll have a dried-up ministry. You may have all the knowledge of theology and the greatest eloquence in your preaching, but you won't have any fruit. The reason is that, in the ministry, whatever is not born of the Spirit is flesh.

From that point on in my life I began to nurture an even greater relationship with the Holy Spirit. I realized that the Holy Spirit had been given to me to work with me, not just to stand in a corner. God is on the throne, and Jesus is at His right hand, but the Spirit is here on earth—in me and in you—to work together with us to bring success to the King's business.

Today I treat the Holy Spirit as the most important Person in my life. I praise Him and I tell Him that I love Him. Then I always say to Him, "Dear Holy Spirit, let's together pray to the Father. Let's together pray to Jesus Christ. Let's together read the Scriptures." Always my fellowship begins with the Holy Spirit. Then with the Holy Spirit I worship God and His Son, Jesus Christ.

So now I feel the presence of the Holy Spirit so intimately that, when the Spirit speaks, I understand. When the Spirit speaks about healing, I understand.

When He speaks about building, I understand. He's such a definite person to me.

Also, I always try to spend at least one hour with the Holy Spirit the first thing every morning. No matter what happens, I want to give Him that one hour. "Dear Holy Spirit," I will say, "let's have a session together. Let's read the Bible together." And so together with the Holy Spirit I sit down and praise God, I worship Jesus and I read the Scriptures. I love the Holy Spirit, and I praise Him, and together we plan the work.

In the early Church the disciples had a definite fellowship with the Holy Spirit—when they had the committee meeting in Jerusalem, for instance. They had been asked to decide on the matter of circumcision of the Gentiles, and in the letter they wrote definitely, "The Holy Spirit and we made this decision, not to lay any extra burden on you . . ." (Acts 15:28, author's paraphrase). They didn't say that the committee had made the decision alone, but *with the Holy Spirit* they decided.

Can we say that in our church meetings? Can we say it in our general councils? When we write down the minutes, do we ever say that "the Holy Spirit and we decided . . ."? No, we don't do that. We see Him only as an overseer in our churches, in our meetings and in our ministry. That's a big mistake.

In our church board meetings at Full Gospel Central Church, the elders and I always pray together, asking the Holy Spirit to come and chair the meeting. The

Holy Spirit is the Senior Partner in our ministry. He's the Chairman of the Board. He's the Main Pastor of the church. We are only the junior pastors.

I also speak in tongues very much. Speaking in tongues is the Holy Spirit's language, and when I speak in tongues, I cannot help but experience His presence in my consciousness. In my own personal prayer life I pray in tongues more than 60 percent of the time. I pray in tongues while I sleep. I wake up praying in tongues. I pray in tongues while I am studying the Bible, and I pray in tongues during my personal devotions. If somehow I ever lost the gift of the tongues, I think my ministry would be whittled down to about 50 percent of what it is now. Whenever I speak in tongues, I cannot help but keep the Holy Spirit in my consciousness.

When I learned to speak English, I began to speak English as much as possible. I began to think in English, and I would write my sermons in English. I would even talk to myself in English, because I really wanted to be proficient in English. For a long time I was tortured, because I was forcing myself to speak in English, but today, although I am not fully fluent in English, I have gained an ease of expression that allows me to speak English without struggling.

Now I am doing the same thing with Japanese—speaking in Japanese, writing in Japanese and even thinking in Japanese—because I have a goal of leading ten million Japanese people to Jesus Christ. For a whole year I have been reading the Japanese Bible, and I have spent so much time in the Japanese language that even in my dreams I am speaking Japanese! In this way I am becoming *acquainted* with the Japanese language. During my waking hours everything in my consciousness is being taken up with Japanese. It has been the same when I have concentrated on English—everything in America and in England and everything in the English-speaking world became my consciousness.

It is the same with speaking in tongues. When you speak in tongues throughout the day, you can't help but be conscious of the presence of the Holy Spirit. Therefore, praying in tongues helps me to have constant fellowship with the Holy Spirit.

Of course, this kind of fellowship with the Holy Spirit signifies a life of prayer. God expects us to be a praying people, because it is through our prayers that God chooses to work in the world today. Powerful, Spirit-inspired prayers work miracles.

All of us need to be saturated with prayer, from the moment we get up in the morning until we go to bed at night. Prayer is our spiritual breathing. If we didn't pray, our spiritual lives would die. But the only real prayer is the kind that can be seen as fellowship with the Holy Spirit, because any other kind of prayer becomes formal and legalistic. God wants us to have intimate fellowship with Him through the Holy Spirit.

Our church is a praying church. It is a church that has real fellowship with the Holy Spirit. We even have regular weekly all-night prayer meetings at the church, and the attendance is usually 10,000 people or more. Prayer is an integral part of the home cell groups meetings. Prayer is the key to revival, both in the church and in the home cell groups.

Not only do we stress prayer at Full Gospel Central Church but we also stress fasting. Many of our cell leaders spend much time in fasting and praying for the salvation of souls in their neighborhoods. Usually they will fast for one to three days. Many have a regular day of fasting every week.

In our congregation I have seen people fasting for seven days if they have a serious problem that God has not solved in answer to simple prayer. If the problem is a matter of life or death, some of our members have fasted for fifteen to twenty days. And a few of our members have even fasted for forty days, just as Jesus did in the wilderness.

But I always tell our people that they must have a goal when they fast. They must not fast just to be fasting, for that accomplishes nothing. When people have been praying for a definite answer and the Lord does not seem to be answering, I tell them to fast and pray until they have the assurance from God that He is answering. In fact, 90 percent of the prayers that have resulted in definite answers in our church have been those prayers that have been combined with fasting.

Each year the members of our church make 300,000 visits to Prayer Mountain. That is our retreat center near the demilitarized zone along our country's border with North Korea. They go there to fast and to pray for special needs. About 60 percent of them go to pray for the baptism in the Holy Spirit and the gift of tongues. The next largest group goes to pray for the solution to family problems, and the third group goes to pray for healing. They have seen many miracles as the result of fasting and praying—there have been healings from cancer and arthritis, for instance, really difficult cases. Others go to pray for business problems or for the salvation of our country, or for revival.

And there are answers! Ninety percent of those who go to Prayer Mountain to fast and pray receive definite answers to their prayers. God is always ready to answer our prayers, but often we pray with the wrong attitude. By fasting and praying, we are telling God we're willing to change our attitudes. Then we become open to praying in accordance with His will, and therefore we will receive the answers He promises.

Fasting and prayer are part of our fellowship with the Holy Spirit. All of us, beginning with the pastor, need to have this kind of prayer life and this kind of fellowship.

13

Motivating Lay Leadership

I have already pointed out that the success of home cell groups depends on the guidance of the pastor, a trained lay leadership and continual fellowship with the Holy Spirit. There is another requirement that I believe is necessary if the cell system is to work smoothly. That requirement is motivation. Good lay leaders need to be motivated.

When a child is born into the world, it hungers for two primary satisfactions: food and a loving touch. If the parents do not supply both of these needs, the child is going to starve, one way or the other. The parents may provide all the food a baby needs for physical nourishment, but if they do not touch the baby, caress him and hug him, then psychologically the child is not going to grow properly. The baby may even die.

Grown-ups too hunger to be touched, to be hugged, to be kissed. They hunger for a loving touch. Without that loving touch, we grown-ups would be starved psychologically. To have a loving home, the husband and wife need to touch each other very often. Friends too need to experience a loving touch: a warm handshake, exuberant back slapping, sometimes a playful punch at each other. It makes them feel alive!

But I want to go beyond this touching of the outward person to show that we human beings also need to be touched inwardly if we are to be motivated to loving action. The pastor and the lay members need to work as a team in providing leadership for home cell groups. The pastors can't carry out all of the heavy work of evangelism to make the church grow, but the lay leaders need to be motivated so that they will undertake their share of the work. That means the pastor needs to know how to touch the inner persons of the lay people so that they will become motivated. Then the pastor can accomplish great things through them.

Here I want to show how to touch the inner person so that the lay people will team up with the pastor in doing the work of evangelism.

To motivate the inner person, we must touch the personality of that person. This is done in three ways:

1. *Recognition.* All people need to be recognized. At Full Gospel Central Church we regularly give certificates as a means of recognizing special achievements among the various kinds of leaders, including the leaders of home cell groups. For instance, I recently signed a

certificate recognizing a Sunday school teacher for eight years of faithful service. That piece of paper hardly cost anything, but with my signature on it, the award shows the Sunday school teacher she has been recognized and appreciated. It really gives her a boost.

And even cell leaders, if they are not recognized frequently, are not going to be motivated to put forth the kind of effort needed to keep evangelism moving in the church. In our church we have a cell leaders convention twice a year. The leaders all come together at the church for a three-day conference, and I speak to them. Now they may not remember all of my lectures to them during those three days, but they will never forget the fact that we care enough about them to give them this much attention. They know they are special people! That is tremendously effective. It motivates them. When it is all over, they have a citation recognizing them for their accomplishments during the preceding six months. They keep that certificate and remember the conference, and they feel important.

This kind of recognition is just as important in the home. A husband should regularly recognize his wife's accomplishments, and likewise the wife should recognize the accomplishments of her husband. A gift of special celebration is always appreciated, and it makes the person being honored feel much more important to his spouse.

Once a month I play golf with the members of our church who are businessmen. Those businessmen contribute a great deal of time, energy, money and leadership to the church. Together we go out to the golf course, and we joke and laugh and slap one another on the back. At the end of the game we have a little meal together. The afternoon of golf can last for four or five hours. During that time I probably will slice or hook the ball into the rough, but we will laugh about it and experience wonderful fellowship. Because we have this special relationship, those businessmen are greatly motivated. They would never think of leaving our church. They are recognized.

I am constantly motivating and recognizing my cell leaders. I motivate them through a weekly cassette message and through closed-circuit television in the church, and I give them frequent recognition in the Sunday services. And, of course, I motivate them through the special seminars. Therefore, all of the cell leaders know they are very special people in our church. They are specially called. They are specially recognized. They are specially liked by their pastor. That motivates them tremendously.

2. *Praise.* We should always try to find out the good qualities or the accomplishments of others and then praise them highly for their characteristics and achievements. That really puts fire into their hearts. If a husband does not know how to praise his wife's cooking, he soon will be starving! And if a wife does not praise her husband for doing a good job working

around the house, he is not going to be motivated very much to do more work.

All of us are born with a hunger for praise. If pastors want to be real leaders in their churches, they must learn how to praise the accomplishments of their lay people. If he doesn't know how to praise them, he does not really have the qualifications for leading them. Without praise, the people will not be motivated.

When it comes to educating our children, we can't motivate them to learn simply by whipping them. At one time in Korea the teacher and the father were greatly feared by the children, and whipping was a kind of negative motivation for the student to achieve a good record in school. But when Western culture began to have an influence on Korea, the children began to have less respect for the teacher and even for their own fathers. The teacher became only a servant.

Even the home life has been affected by westernization. The wives used to obey their husbands; nowadays there is pressure for equal rights, just like in America.

In the society we have today, the best way to motivate anyone is not to find fault with him but to look for his good points and to praise him for those. It's better to look for good points and good traits and to overlook the faults. By praising people for their good points you will be helping them to correct their faults.

Praising is the best way of motivation, even in Christian work. I try my best to praise people in our church—the pastors under me, the elders, the deacons and deaconesses, and the cell leaders. Any time anyone does an especially good job, I make sure he is recognized and praised for it. I will give him a slap on the back and say, "My, how were you able to do this? It's wonderful! It's fantastic!"

When all this is done with real sincerity, shown in the tone of voice and in the facial expression, accompanied by a slap on the back, that person will remember it for a year! That's the way it works in our church.

3. *Love.* To motivate people, we need to give them genuine love, which is evident by the expression on our face, the tone of our voice and the way we act. People really respond to genuine love. I respond to love. When I step on the platform of Full Gospel Central Church, I can really feel love radiating from the people in the congregation. Our people love me so much that I become very motivated, and I try my very best to help them. I will never neglect them and I will never forget them.

I also love the people very much, and they know it. I don't even have to say it, but I feel it, and the people are touched by the unseen rays of love from me. It's a genuine love, with genuine concern for their benefit.

To sum up, I always follow these three guidelines in motivating people in our church: (1) *Recognition.* If I show them they are important people, they will never feel inferior. If they ever begin to feel inferior, they will develop an inferiority complex, and then they will be washed up and so will my church. (2) *Praise.* Praising puts oil and fire into their hearts. (3) *Love.* I give them genuine love.

The people of Full Gospel Central Church are motivated people, and they are trying their best to work for the Lord.

When I go home in the evening, if my wife is not there, I always wait for her. I will not eat dinner without her. Even if I feel starved, I wait until she comes. Then when she gets home she will say, "Why are you waiting? Why didn't you eat?"

And I say, "Oh, honey, I have no taste for food if you are not here."

My wife feels as though she is the queen in my home, because I recognize her, I praise her and I show her genuine love. No wife is ever going to leave a husband who treats her like that. "He needs me," she will say. "He can't live without me."

In Korea about 50 percent of the husbands cheat on their wives. The reason, I have heard again and again, is that they are not recognized. "Oh, my wife does not appreciate me," the husband will say. "I go someplace where I'm recognized and appreciated. I want to feel like somebody."

Too many wives are losing their husbands because they take them for granted. By the same token, many husbands are also losing their wives for the same reason. Everybody needs to feel important—every day, every hour, every minute. It's a psychological need.

Therefore, we need to recognize each other in our homes—and in our churches and home cell groups.

If we can show recognition to one another, praising one another and showing genuine love to one another, all of us will become motivated to accomplish big things.

Many people can organize, and they can organize beautifully. But an organization, no matter how beautifully it is put together, is not going to work properly if the people in it are not properly motivated to do the work.

I mentioned earlier that one church in the United States went to great lengths to organize a system of home cell groups. I even went there to help them set it up. But it was not too long until the system began to flounder. The reason was that the pastor had turned everything over to one of his associates, and he had no further direct input. Then when the system began to flounder, he came to me and asked what had gone wrong. As he shared the problems with me, I saw immediately what was wrong.

"Even though you felt that cell groups were very important to the life of your church," I said, "you did not demonstrate that concern to your congregation. You turned everything over to one of your associates, and you had nothing further to do with it. To your congregation, cell groups didn't seem very important to you. The leaders were not motivated to carry on."

In our church I will never turn over the leadership of

the cell system to one of my associates. I am the leader. Every Wednesday afternoon I am motivating the leaders through the television system in the church. Twice a year I personally lead the cell leaders' seminars. I never allow anyone else to lead those meetings. I am always there, and the people see that I consider them important.

A number of other churches have also failed in trying to establish home cell groups because the pastor was not directly involved. I always tell pastors who attend my church growth seminars that, if they do not take charge personally, their cell leaders and their members are not going to be motivated, and the system will fail.

If the pastor really takes charge of the home cell groups if he takes an active part in organizing them, and if he trains the leadership and constantly motivates them, the people are going to be on fire. They will see that it's important. They will work hard and do a good job.

Then the home cell groups will succeed and the church will really begin to grow.

14

Preaching to a Growing Church

I have mentioned several prerequisites for establishing a strong, growing church based on home cell groups. They are fellowship with the Holy Spirit, delegation of authority to a group of lay leaders, and the training and motivation of those leaders. Now I would like to discuss one further consideration: preaching.

That subject may seem like an obvious one to some readers, but it is not as simple as it appears. The style of one's preaching will often determine whether home cell groups will result in a growing church.

In chapter 12 I have already mentioned my dependence upon the Holy Spirit. Close fellowship with the Holy Spirit is essential. It is through His intimate presence in our lives that we receive the inspiration and anointing to bring the message needed by our congregation at every service.

Through my fellowship with the Holy Spirit I feel a

real anointing when I go out to preach. Oh, what a difference that anointing makes! It is especially necessary in the expository sermons I give at Wednesday night meetings and at the Friday all-night prayer meetings in Full Gospel Central Church.

When I began to teach the Bible verse-by-verse on Wednesday evenings, beginning with Genesis and intending to go through the whole Bible to the end of Revelation, some people told me attendance would be very small.

"On Sundays when you preach a topical message, people will come," they said, "but if you teach verse by verse, everyone will lose interest."

"Yes, you're right," I said. "If I just teach the Bible verse by verse according to my own knowledge, nobody will want to listen. But if I go to the platform together with the Holy Spirit, they will come because they will listen to Him."

So I depended upon the Holy Spirit and launched forth. Sometimes I would teach for two and three hours at a time, yet the people seemed to sit there spellbound. Not only did the people grow more in grace, but they were actually enjoying it!

Now I realize that in some of the chapters I become very tedious. Particularly when you study such books as Leviticus, and you have to teach verse by verse on all those minute requirements of the Jewish law, you feel like dying! But still you must teach it to the people, because all of the Bible is important to their spiritual growth.

As I have come to depend more and more on the Holy Spirit, both in my topical sermons on Sundays and in my expository teachings on week nights, I rely less and less on philosophy and the knowledge of history that I learned in Bible school and in my early days of ministry. After twenty-three years of preaching I have found that only the Word of God quickens people. At one time I preached almost like a philosopher, and I became very profound, but at the same time I was making very few converts.

Now I have become very simple—ignorant, perhaps—in worldly ways, but I have become very profound in Scripture. As I relied solely on the Bible, I began to have more and more converts, including the more intellectual people of the city. Teaching the Bible under the anointing of the Holy Spirit is very powerful

In my preaching I also have a definite goal. I don't simply preach at random. My goal is always to help people meet Jesus Christ personally—every Sunday, every Wednesday night, every Friday night and every other time I am called to preach. Each sermon is focused so that people will meet Jesus Christ through it. If they are unbelievers, let them meet Jesus Christ and be converted; if they are already believers, let them meet Jesus Christ and become more profound in their faith. If I miss the bull's-eye there, the sermon is a failure.

My second goal in preaching is to help people succeed in life—in spirit, soul, body and business. As the people of my congregation become successful in their home lives, as they become successful in their business lives or careers, and as they become successful in their relationships with other people, then I also become successful. As much as I want to become a successful minister, to that same extent I try to make the people of my congregation successful. My own success is a secondary goal. The people must succeed first.

Finally, the goal of my preaching is to help people serve God and other people in a greater way. Once people meet Jesus Christ and become successful in their own lives, they should use the power and the success of their newfound relationship with Christ to serve God and other people with spiritual energy, mental energy and physical energy—and with an abundance of finances. (I don't apologize for financial success, because it is a means of serving God and helping others. Our own church budget is large enough that we can really move into evangelization, not only in Korea but also in Japan, the United States, Europe and elsewhere. In fact, this kind of success among our people is a miracle, because we are citizens of a Third World country. To tell the truth, if they were not successful, we could not afford to carry on the big program we have. At Full Gospel Central Church we do not talk about depression, oil shortages or other such difficulties. While other businesses are slowing down, our people are becoming prosperous, even in the midst of severe inflation and economic depression, which is what we have had in Korea in 1980. Yet the offering continues to increase every Sunday in our church.)

In all of my sermons, whether in Korea, Japan, the United States or Europe, I always have three goals: to introduce people to Jesus Christ, to make them successful and to motivate them to serve God and their fellow man. Then I have a sure foundation as a minister.

Now where, you might ask, do I begin in my preaching? I always begin with the goodness of God. That is the most important theology.

Until I was nineteen years old, I was a Buddhist—really a devout Buddhist. I thought Buddhism was the best religion in the world. Theoretically (in terms of theology) Buddhism is very profound. But whenever I went to the temple, I always felt frightened of those idols. I always prayed, asking the Buddha not to punish me. My whole relationship with the Buddhist religion was based on a ritualism and responsibility rooted in fear. In the Buddhist faith, my faith was born in fear, not in love. The god of Buddha was not a god of love but one of judgment.

When I became a Christian, Jesus Christ not only saved my soul but He also healed me of tuberculosis and raised me up from my deathbed. Then when I was baptized in the Holy Spirit, the love of God began to pour like a river into my soul. The greatest things I experienced as a Christian were the love of God and the goodness of God.

God has really been good to me. When I came to Him

I was very poor. I was a dropout from my first year in high school. My father could not afford to send me to school any longer, and I had been weak with tuberculosis. I seemingly had no future. But through my newfound relationship with Jesus Christ, and by reading the Bible, I equipped myself with a positive faith. Through that, God pulled me out of that whole miserable situation. He gave me all the health, wealth, knowledge, victory and everything I needed. Everything I have has come from God.

Because of my relationship with God, because I know Him as a good God, a loving Father, that is the God I preach. Yet I have met so many people who tell me that they have had a wrathful, vengeful God preached to them, and they had great difficulty relating to a loving, good God.

Not too long ago I was preaching in Germany when a woman came to me and asked me to pray for her and her husband. She had a tremendous fear of God which had been brought on when her parents had been killed in a bombing raid in World War II. Now her husband was despondent with severe neurotic depression, and she was afraid she would lose him just the way she had lost her father and mother.

I began to tell her about the goodness of God, how He had created the world and had found it good. "He is the God who tried to bring good to the sin and sickness of the world by giving us His Son, Jesus Christ," I told her. "That God is a good God, and that God is your

Father and my Father.

"Change your thinking," I said, "and begin to see God as a good God. Praise Him and tell Him, 'I love you, Father. You're a good God, and you want me to have goodness in my life.' "

"I'm scared," she said. "No one has ever taught me that way before."

"Well, I'm teaching you right now," I said. "Don't be scared. Just change your image of God."

Then she began to repeat after me, "God is a good God. He's my good Father. He wants to give good things to His children. He's good. He's good."

Soon she felt the release and began to laugh, and not long after that her husband was completely freed of his neurotic oppression.

I believe that when we preach a good God we get people released from bondage. Bondage comes from the enemy. The devil uses wrong theology to try to bring people under the bondage of fear and desolation. Many preachers have taught their people only to fear the God of judgment, and they have told them not to expect anything from Him.

I am a father. I have three boys, and I do everything to bring goodness to my children. Yet the Bible says, "If you, then, though you are evil, know how to give good gifts to your children, how much more will your Father in heaven give good gifts to those who ask him!" (Matt. 7:11, NIV).

It's very, very hard to persuade some Christians to

think of God in this way, because they think they always have to suffer and struggle to be good Christians. They feel we should constantly go through trials and live a poverty-stricken life to be good Christians. Well, if our suffering brings any redeeming grace to other people, then I believe that suffering is justified.

The Bible says that we should suffer together with Jesus Christ, but did Jesus Christ ever suffer from sin? Did He ever suffer from sickness? Did He ever suffer the oppression of Satan? No, He never suffered from any of those things. Did He ever suffer from poverty? Yes, He did, but in a redeeming way, as it says in 2 Cor. 8:9, "Though he was rich, yet for your sakes he became poor, so that you through his poverty might become rich" (NIV).

If the Bible commands us to suffer together with Jesus Christ, that suffering should not be because of sin, sickness, the devil, a curse or poverty. Then from what did Jesus suffer? Persecution. He only suffered for the sake of the gospel, because of persecution. Therefore, neither should we accept suffering except by persecution. And if that suffering does not bring any redeeming result, then that suffering is for nothing.

I don't think I can ever become poor. I would gladly suffer poverty if it brought any redeeming grace to the people, but I have found that trying to become poor is the most difficult thing in my life. When I was building the new church on Yoido Island, I gave up everything— even my home. But the more I gave up, the more God returned to me! That's according to the Bible. So now I've given up. I have no hope of becoming poor.

Now if God sent the Communists to take over our country, and I suffered because of that, that would be suffering caused by persecution, and it would be justified. Or if a person volunteers to become a missionary, and he gives up his home and the comforts of Western society to bring Jesus Christ to people in the jungles of New Guinea, then his suffering will be for the cause of redemption. He is suffering the lack of all the conveniences of civilization, but it is for a purpose.

Therefore, the foundation of my sermons is the goodness of God. Next to that I preach on the blood of Jesus Christ. I always base my sermon and my faith on the blood of Christ, for without the blood of Jesus Christ there can be no redemption. Without redemption there is no reason to persist in one's faith.

Jesus shed His blood in four places, the first of them being the Garden of Gethsemane. There His perspiration fell like big drops of blood, and it had a special meaning to those being redeemed. He shed His blood as He was saying, "Not my will but thine be done." The first Adam disobeyed God to persist in his own will. But the last Adam, Jesus Christ, in the Garden of Gethsemane was offering himself and offering up the will of mankind in obedience to God. As the high priest of the people He was offering up their own disobedient will and He redeemed it.

We can say very definitely that God's Holy Spirit can

help us to obey God's will, because the blood of Jesus Christ speaks even today. The blood redeems our disobedience, which we inherited from our father, the first Adam.

The second time Jesus shed His blood was when the crown of thorns was placed upon His head. The thorns cut into His head, and blood gushed out. What does that blood represent? It symbolizes the curse. When Adam and Eve fell from grace, the Bible says that the earth was cursed and would produce thorns and thistles. The thorn is the symbol of the curse. But by shedding His blood, Jesus redeemed His people from the curse.

Today so many people, including Christians, are living in the thorny patch of hatred, fear and inferiority. But the blood of Jesus Christ speaks against that curse, for by it we are redeemed from the curse.

The third time Jesus shed His blood was at the whipping post. The Roman soldiers took off His clothes and laid stripe upon stripe upon His back until it was completely torn, and blood gushed out and streamed down. Here He shed His blood to bring us healing, for the Bible says, "With his stripes we are healed" (Isa. 53:5). We cannot ignore that in our preaching, for that blood still speaks today.

Finally, Jesus shed His blood on the cross at Calvary, when the Roman soldier thrust a spear into His side. Out gushed blood and water, and the shedding of that blood redeemed us totally from sin and death.

Therefore, without the shedding of blood there would

be no redemption. Without the blood we have no foundation to preach against Satan. But once we build our messages on the foundation of the blood of Jesus Christ, then we have tremendous grounds for proclaiming victory over Satan. I base my sermons on the blood of Jesus Christ and build the faith of the people in my congregation so that they will not fear anything. I put faith into their hearts!

When our people leave the church and return to their homes and businesses, they do not live only by their own circumstances, but they live by faith. The Bible says, "The righteous shall live by faith," and "Be it according to your faith." If we do not build faith into the people, they have nothing to claim for victory. They have faith only by way of the minister's message. If the minister gives them only a shaky faith, the devil will come along and destroy that rickety faith. But if the faith is founded on the blood of Jesus Christ, the devil can't stand it.

Then, after basing my sermons on the goodness of God and on redemption through the blood of Jesus Christ, I build on the foundation of a successful life. It is a sure biblical principle—from Genesis to Revelation. The principle of success is demonstrated so many times. If you want to have financial success in your business, then you should apply the principle of sowing and reaping, for the Bible says, "Give, and it shall be given unto you; good measure, pressed down, and shaken together, and running over, shall men give into your bosom" (Luke 6:38). And how do you keep your home life happy and healthy? By keeping Sunday holy, not doing any work, worshiping God together with the family. And how can you have business success? Apply the principles of faith in the eleventh chapter of Hebrews.

So I teach all of these principles of success to the people in our church, and they apply them to their lives, just as we in the church leadership apply the principles of church growth through home cell groups. And the people are successful! Therefore I have no need for trying to become eloquent—in fact, I have no intention of ever becoming eloquent—because I have turned my pulpit into a counseling place.

The method of preaching, then, is to counsel the people to help them meet their needs. People are always coming to church in great need, but if the preacher is only talking about theology, history and politics, the people are not going to be helped in their personal lives, where they need the message. They will be dozing off instead.

One day I was returning to Korea from the United States, and I stopped over in Japan for one day. I was afraid that if I got back to Korea on Saturday I would have to labor in the pulpit the next day, so I had a very good excuse to take a one-day vacation.

I decided to go to a Japanese Christian church that Sunday, and the one I attended turned out to have a minister who used very big words. He did not have just a five-dollar vocabulary; he had a ten-dollar vocabulary. There are many ministers like that, and not just in Japan. They feel that the larger their vocabularies are the greater their ministries become. What those ministers do not realize is that their congregations understand less than 50 percent of their preaching. Then, if the congregation does not understand what the minister has said, they may say, "My, isn't our minister profound? Isn't he erudite?" But when you ask them, "What did he preach about?" they are unable to tell you.

Well, the minister in the Japanese church I attended that Sunday was one of the leading ministers in Japan. Yet I sat there squirming and uncomfortable, feeling that if the hour were not over soon I would die. He was not meeting the need of my heart—or of his people! Instead, he was discussing international politics, using those ten-dollar words I could not understand.

That is the trouble with many churches in Japan— and the reason people are not going to the Japanese churches. Why should they go to a Christian church that does not speak to their needs or to the cries of their hearts? No wonder a Japanese church considers itself fortunate to have 100 members!

I try desperately to relate all of my sermons to the needs of the people. In one series of sermons, for instance, I preached on "How to Win Over Depression." People are constantly talking about depression, as well as business difficulties and financial troubles. So when I preach to bring them success in those areas, people are coming to the church and sitting in the aisles to hear the sermon. Others are standing in the back of the church and filling the gymnasium and several chapels, where they can watch on closed-circuit television. (Our church seats 10,000 people, but usually 15,000 squeeze in for each of the six services we have every Sunday.) They know the sermon will be concerned with the solution to their problems.

I also try to be relevant to contemporary life. Many young people are leaving other churches, feeling that the sermons and the programs are not relevant to them. They say, "We'll come back when we're sixty years old and the sermons are relevant to us. Then we can prepare for heaven, because that's all the ministers seem to be preaching about—getting ready for heaven. But we are living on earth now, and the message is unrelated to our lives."

People generally judge sermons according to their own personal interests. They are interested in loss or gain to themselves. They are asking, "What do I gain from this sermon?" If the sermon addresses their needs, if they really get something from it for their personal lives, they will come and listen even if there is no air conditioning in the church building or no heating system.

You see people going to the stock market no matter what the weather, no matter what the inconvenience, and they stand there staring at the lights that quote the buying and selling prices of the stocks in which they are interested. They are very interested—sometimes desperately interested—in whether they have lost or gained something.

That is the same way people judge our sermons. They are not interested in eloquence, but only in whether they might gain or lose anything.

Finally, I try in all of my sermons to uplift the people in some way. I try to instill faith, hope and love in them. I try to teach them how to be successful Christians. I never pound them down. Often when a new Bible school graduate comes into our church to preach, the first thing he does is condemn the people and pummel them with judgmental theology. Then he says to himself, "What a great message I preached!"

But that is not our purpose as ministers. We are not here to condemn the people but to uplift them and lead them into righteousness. The Mosaic law was given to condemn the people, but the grace of Jesus Christ was given to redeem the people. The worst sermon is one of condemnation. The easiest sermon is one of condemnation. Using the sword of the Ten Commandments, one can condemn a person very easily. But our job is to uplift people by putting faith, hope and love into their hearts. They want to know how to be successful Christians, successful fathers, successful mothers, husbands, wives, businessmen—through Jesus Christ.

That is my philosophy, and I believe it also is the philosophy of the Bible. Of course, I speak against sin—although not in a condemning way but in a constructive way. I say that if you live in sin you are going to hell, but I always show them the answer: how to come out of their sin through the blood of Jesus Christ. I never leave our congregation with a feeling of condemnation.

In America, Dr. Robert Schuller has a great audience all across the country. The reason is that he is always preaching on "possibility thinking," putting faith, hope and love into the hearts of his listeners. When I am in the United States and am in a hotel room somewhere on a Sunday, and want to watch a Christian program on television, I turn to Dr. Schuller's "Hour of Power." I know I can depend on him to put faith, hope and love into my heart. His sermons uplift me.

I have listened to some other preachers, including some very well-known evangelists, and when I hear them I turn off the program. They keep condemning the people, and I feel so depressed that I don't even feel like praying. Such preaching makes of little account the blood of Jesus Christ, which has redeemed us from sin.

That is why I preach on faith, hope and love. I know I am preaching to the needs of the people, and the sermons are uplifting them.

This is my preaching style and this is my life. So far it has proven very successful, not only in Korea but in other parts of the world as well. I can preach for one, two or even three hours, and the people will sit spell-bound. Why? Because the sermon meets their needs. It is relevant to them, to their contemporary lives. I uplift them, putting faith, hope and love into their hearts. People listen, because they feel they have something tremendous to gain by listening to my sermons. They stay and pay attention.

15

The Possibility of
Church Growth Unlimited

This book would not be complete if I did not share
one thing more on how to use these principles to make
a church really grow. Although I have mentioned this
in another of my books, *The Fourth Dimension,* it is
especially appropriate that I share it here as well.

A minister may have adopted all of the principles I
have enumerated here—delegating authority and forming home cell groups, being in constant fellowship
with the Holy Spirit, motivating his lay leadership and
preaching meaningful sermons—and still fall far short
of the unlimited church growth we have experienced at
Full Gospel Central Church.

In this final chapter I would like to show how to put
it all together so you will have church growth unlimited.
This is the very reason so many pastors are coming to
Korea to study our church, and it is the reason I am
invited to seminars all over the world. The pastors are

asking, "How can I make my church grow like that?"

The number-one requirement for having real church growth—unlimited church growth—is to set goals. Of course, that may seem obvious, but the real determining factor is the way we apply this principle. Unfortunately it is possible to set goals in the wrong way and then put in a great deal of self-effort in exhorting the lay leaders to bring in new members. Some growth may be realized in this way, but it will eventually reach a plateau. The church growth I am talking about (and our church is experiencing) will have no plateaus.

When I began my ministry in 1958, I knew nothing about goal setting. So I used all kinds of gimmicks to bring in new members. They did not work. For the first six months I did not lead even one soul to Jesus Christ. During that time I became very frustrated, so much so that eight times I decided to pack up and leave my ministry. It was only through the encouragement of the Reverend Jashil Choi, the woman who was later to become my mother-in-law, that I was sustained.

Then God showed me, by the intervention of the Holy Spirit, that I should establish clear-cut goals, not only to build a growing church but also to form a victorious personal prayer life. At that time I was very, very poor. I had almost no income, and I was living from hand to mouth. Often I would fast simply because I didn't have anything to eat.

One day I was reading the Bible when suddenly I was really encouraged to ask for and expect to receive what

I needed from God by faith. Until then I had learned in Bible school only that we could ask to be saved through the blood of Jesus Christ.

At that time the greatest necessities in my life were a table, a chair and a bicycle. So I knelt down and asked God to give me those three things, and I really prayed with great faith. Then I waited for God to supply them. Day after day, month after month, I waited, expecting. But nothing happened.

Eventually, completely frustrated, discouraged and despondent, I cried out to the Lord. Then God began to speak to me. It was the first time God ever spoke to me that I was certain I heard Him. I still do not know whether it was in an audible voice or by an impression in my spirit. I know I saw a bright light, and I did receive the message.

God said, *"My son, don't cry. I have heard your prayer, and I have given you a table, a chair and a bicycle."*

So I said, "Father, you're kidding me. I don't have a table, a chair or a bicycle, although I have been expecting them day after day."

"Yes," God said, *"I have given them to you potentially. But you have been asking them of me in such vague terms that I cannot fulfill your request. Don't you know there are a dozen kinds of tables, a dozen kinds of chairs and a dozen kinds of bicycles? Which ones do you want? Be very clear. I have so much trouble with my children, because they keep asking me and asking*

me and asking me, yet they themselves do not know what kind of thing they want. Make your request very specific, and then I'll answer."

So I said, "Father, prove that to me by the Scriptures."

Then the Spirit told me to open the Bible to Hebrews 11, and I did, beginning to read from the first verse: "Now faith is the substance of things hoped for. . . ."

Immediately my eyes fell on the word *things.* Then the Spirit said to me, "Without having a clear-cut goal of the 'things,' or a clear-cut vision of the objects, how can you hope? How do you have faith?"

Then Scripture after Scripture began to flow into my mind, all telling me I should always have a clear-cut goal. For instance, when Jesus was on the road to Jericho, He was approached by a blind man, Bartimaeus. Now Jesus and everybody else knew what Bartimaeus wanted—to be healed of his blindness. But Jesus clearly asked the question, " 'What do you want me to do for you?' And the blind man said to Him, 'Rabboni, I want to regain my sight!'

"And Jesus said to him, 'Go your way; your faith has made you well' " (Mark 10:51-52, NASB).

Time and again I saw in Scripture that Jesus asked specific questions, expecting goal-oriented answers. And throughout Scripture God did miracles in response to clear-cut requests with specific goals in mind.

So I began to make a specific request in my prayer, describing the size and type of table I wanted, made of

Philippine mahogany, with an iron-frame chair on casters that would enable me to roll around. Then I asked for an American-made bicycle with a gearshift on the side. I went into specific detail in my request.

And I believed! In a few months I received *all* of those things exactly as I had requested. That caused a tremendous truth to dawn upon me. I realized I had prayed daily for revival, but still I had an empty church. Yet I had asked for a table, a chair and a bicycle, and I got exactly what I had asked for. Could God be more concerned about a table, chair and bicycle than about the salvation of souls?

I realized I had had a wrong attitude about building the church, just as I had had a wrong attitude about prayer. I had asked God for blessings, expecting Him to shower them down upon me, but the blessings had not come because I had not been specific in my requests until I asked for that table, chair and bicycle. Then I learned that God would answer my prayers only through my own dreams, visions and faith.

I knew God was within me by the Holy Spirit, which meant He was not going to bring the answers to me from beyond me, but those answers were going to bubble up from within me.

Today I know that the capacity for God's answer depends on the size of the pipe in which we give Him the opportunity to work. If the size of my pipe is small, the blessings are only going to trickle down; but if through faith I have increased the size of that pipe, the blessings will pour down.

At that time I had the capacity for believing for only 150 members. I thought at that time that I would be eternally satisfied with that many people in my church. So I set a very clear goal of 150 members, and I wrote it down on a paper and put it up on my wall. I also wrote the number on other slips of paper and put them everywhere, including in my wallet. Everywhere I turned I saw the number 150. Eventually I was completely saturated with it.

I began to eat with 150. I slept with the number 150 in my dreams. I was living with 150 members in my heart, although I still did not have more than a few actual members in my congregation. After a while I began to preach as though I were speaking to 150 people, and I walked like a pastor who had 150 members.

Before the first year was over, I had those 150 members! For six months I had struggled without leading one soul to Christ, but in the second six months, when I had a clear-cut goal and began really to believe, then God answered my prayers and brought the 150 members.

But after I had them I was not satisfied with only 150 members. Who would be satisfied with that number? So the second year I set a goal of 300, and I got 300. The next year I set a goal of 300 more, and by the end of 1961 I had 600 members. Then we moved the church to West Gate with a goal of 3,000 members by 1964. That was when I got into trouble, because I was not organized to handle 3,000, and I collapsed under the strain when the number reached 2,400.

It should be obvious by now that both principles need to be applied to the church if it is going to grow in an unlimited way: (1) We need to have a vision, or goal, and (2) we need to delegate authority to lay leaders by establishing home cell groups.

When we moved to Yoido Island and built the present Full Gospel Central Church, I set a goal of 30,000 members, because I did not think I could successfully pastor any more than that. But when I got 30,000, I knew I could handle even more. So I asked for 50,000, then 70,000, and by the end of 1979 our church had reached the goal of 100,000 members. That was a real landmark, but still I knew we could handle more.

In fact, my goal is now for 500,000 members by 1984. I can believe for that number, because I can grasp that vision very clearly. We have added 50,000 members in 1980, and it should be no trouble to add 70,000 more in 1981. Then in 1982 we'll add 100,000 more, and in 1983 we'll add 200,000.

All of this happens with no fanfare, no special outreach campaigns. I simply set a goal, and then I ask God for it specifically. I believe with real faith, and the cell leaders do the rest.

In addition to the principle of setting goals, there are

four other principles that go along with it. These are all very closely related.

The second of these principles is dreaming. You have to have a goal, yes. But if you don't dream, you will never reach that goal. A dream (or vision) is the basic material the Holy Spirit uses to build anything for you. The Bible says, "Where there is no vision, the people perish" (Prov. 29:18). When you don't have a vision, you don't produce anything.

Dreams and visions are the basic material with which the Holy Spirit works. I always say that visions and dreams are the language of the Holy Spirit. If you don't speak the language, you won't produce anything. The Holy Spirit wants to communicate with us, but if we don't have dreams and visions, He can't communicate with us. In the Bible, whenever God wanted to do anything for anybody, first He put visions and dreams into their hearts. When Abraham was seventy-five years old, God gave him a vision of being the father of many nations. When he was 100 years old, Abraham was ready to have that vision fulfilled. God called him out and let him count the stars in the sky, because He wanted Abraham to visualize the number of his children, which would be "as numerous as the stars of the sky."

Before Joseph was sold into slavery in Egypt, God had already put visions and dreams into his heart. Through those visions and dreams God eventually overruled all the circumstances that had occurred in

Joseph's life, making him even prime minister of Egypt.

When I was in the first stage of my pioneering work, God told me to dream. As I knelt down to pray, the Spirit told me to dream: *"Dream the largest church in Korea."* I was in a dilapidated tent church, but God said, *"Dream!"* From then on I learned to live in a visionary world. When I began to dream that the church was packed with people, people began to pour into the church. Without the Holy Spirit, that would be impossible, but the Holy Spirit was using my dreams to bring the people in.

Dreaming seems foolish to the rational mind, and I would agree, if dreaming is done without goals. But when you establish a goal and begin to dream for that goal, that dream becomes creative. The Holy Spirit uses it to bring the future to the present!

Today the pastors in Korea who have the largest churches apply my principles. I have taught them to use the principles of forming home cell groups, setting goals and dreaming. Except for the Presbyterian church, which is the second largest church with 36,000 members, the largest churches are mostly all pastored by those who have learned my principles. One has 12,000 members and another has 10,000. And whenever we get together, I always tell them, "Keep on dreaming. You are going to grow only as big as your dream."

I am constantly living in a world of God-given

dreams. Today I am living with 500,000 members inside me. Those potential members are like 500,000 eggs that I am incubating in my spirit. By 1984 all of those eggs will have hatched!

God can fill us only to our own capacity, and for me, my capacity has really grown, because of those visions and dreams.

Third, we must believe. We must really believe we are going to get what we ask for, what we are dreaming for. And we must speak the believing word. We must never, never speak in negative terms ("I can't do it. I have no finances. I don't have the strength"). If we are depending on the Holy Spirit, we are not depending on our own resources. We are depending on God's resources.

Therefore, once we have a goal, once we dream that goal into reality and are pregnant with the answer to our prayer, then we must speak it. I am constantly speaking about those 500,000 members, persuading myself completely in my mind and in my faith.

The fourth thing a pastor must do in order to produce church growth is to persuade the congregation of the reality of that goal and get some enthusiasm started. By constantly speaking about my goal and my visions, I am generating enthusiasm in the people and persuading them that it is going to happen. I cannot build a big church by myself. I need the cooperation of all the members of our congregation—they join their hearts with mine to believe for the growth. I talk about the goal with my associates, and I speak about it to the deacons and deaconesses. I speak about it to the women's association and to the men's fellowship. I speak about it to everyone at all possible times. By speaking thus, I am releasing power, as it says in the Bible: "If anyone says to this mountain, 'Go, throw yourself into the sea,' and does not doubt in his heart but believes that what he says will happen, it will be done for him" (Mark 11:23, NIV). If that speaking is joined to the voices of the congregation, that power becomes multiplied.

Lastly, we must get ready. Many people desire growth, but they never get ready for it. When growth suddenly begins, what are they going to do? How can they be prepared for growth if they have not already begun raising funds for a larger church building? When we believe for growth, and when that growth becomes real to us in our dreams, then we need to act as though we already have that growth.

I have already begun construction of a fifteen-story church building next to the present Full Gospel Central Church. The building will cost $10 million. The center of the building will be open all the way up to the fifteenth floor, and all of the floors will be equipped with closed-circuit television so that everyone will be able to see what is going on. Right now I don't have enough members to fill it, but in my imagination there are that many members. So I have taken the risk and I am building.

If I were not ready for growth, then what would I do with all the new members that will be coming to the church as the revival gains momentum? If I'm not prepared, I will be losing many of them, because they will not be able to find a place in church on Sunday.

After that building is completed, I am going to build a whole new church complex surrounding and enclosing the present church building. Then we will knock out the walls of the inner building to join it to the outer one. I will spend another $10 million for that.

I am also enlarging Prayer Mountain to seat 5,000 people, because as the church grows we will see more people going to Prayer Mountain. There I will spend another $3 million.

Where do I get all the money? God is my resource. When I built the present structure on Yoido Island, I started with a goal and with my visions and dreams, but I had only $2,500. The projected cost of the building at that time was $2 million. God saw me through. Now it is not too difficult for me to believe for $23 million for these new projects.

When people catch the vision and become enthusiastic, finances are the last thing to worry about. Always when I begin a new project, my calculator is the last thing I reach for. The first thing I ask is, "Is this the will of the Lord?" If yes, then, "Do we have a clear-cut goal? Can we conquer that goal and possess it in our visions and dreams? Do we really believe? Do we really have the enthusiasm of the people?"

If the answer to all of those questions is yes, then I have to get ready. That is the time to reach for my calculator and determine the cost. Then I assume the money is going to come, and I go ahead by faith and walk on the water. I don't see the wind or the waves; I just go on.

We must show to the world that we really believe. If we wait until the growth comes, we will be working two to three years behind schedule to accommodate it, and we will lose many members along the way. This kind of ministry takes risky faith.

It would be ridiculous for a pregnant woman to say, "Well, if I am going to give birth to a child, I will wait until it happens, and then I will buy some baby clothes and a crib." There would be something lacking in such a woman.

It is just the same when we are giving birth to church growth. It comes about because that growing church is inside us. We are pregnant with it, by the power of the Holy Spirit. That is the only way it will be born. The church is not just going to be *built,* it is going to be *born.* What I am doing at our church in Seoul is building a larger crib. I want to be ready.

For a minister who is interested in church growth—real church growth—this kind of thinking is a twenty-four-hour-a-day business. It's not something that is relegated to Sunday or to a few meetings. It is pregnant within the pastor. Growing a church (or birthing a church) in this fashion can be done anywhere, and the minister does not even have to be at the church all the time for it to happen. He can be 1,000 miles away or more, and it will still go on. I am often thousands of miles away from home, and I am traveling overseas up to six months of the year. But the growth of our church does not depend on my physical presence. It depends on the capacity of my dreaming and my faith— wherever I am.

With such a capacity and such faith a minister can build this kind of church anywhere. It can be in New York, in Los Angeles, or New Orleans or Dallas. People who have studied with me have started churches all over the world following these principles, including fifty in the United States, ten in Europe and three in Japan. Every one of them has become self-supporting within six months, and many of them are already sending out missionaries. The traditional view of missionary work sees this as impossible. But my disciples have proved it can be done—even in Bangkok, which is a very poor area.

Today the heathens are no longer in some far-off jungle. We live in a very small world because of the jet airplane. In thirty hours we can get anywhere on the globe. And the "heathen" countries are no longer "out there." There are heathens everywhere. There are heathens in the United States, heathens in Europe, and heathens in Korea and Japan. We are all living in a heathen world that needs to hear the gospel of Jesus Christ.

This is totally opposite to the traditional view of missions, which sees only the heathen world as some place far off, needing Western missionaries to go out preaching the gospel, supported by their home churches. When we turn that perspective of missionary work around and look at it from the viewpoint of the heathens, we see those missionaries as a source of wealth, because they will be bringing in money. That's what many heathens see—money and opportunity. But very seldom do they see and understand the gospel.

That is why I don't give my missionaries money to give to the heathens. I support them for six months, and after that they're on their own. I tell them, "I'm sending you out to give them the gospel, and only the gospel. Don't give them any impression that you are bringing them riches. You can only help them genuinely by giving them the gospel. Don't worry about the money. Those things will take care of themselves."

When people say they can't become missionaries because they don't have money, they have a false idea about the ability of God to provide. I started my ministry totally broke in a dilapidated tent church, but I never depended upon any foreign missionary for support. I purposely avoided receiving any foreign financial aid. I have since given tens of thousands of dollars for missionary work overseas, including in the

United States and Europe.

God must be our total resource. If we depend on any other source, we will have no one to turn to when shortages come. I determined to make God my total resource, and He has never failed me. In twenty-three years I have built three churches, and God has supplied all of my needs.

Now our church has sent out seventy-five missionaries all over the world, and they have learned that same lesson. God will supply all of our needs when we depend on Him as our total resource.

Therefore, we should all be encouraged that church growth is possible if we follow the principles I have related in this book. Church growth comes by the Holy Spirit, by the Word of God and by pastors of faith. Using the system of home cell groups, we can build a church anywhere.

Suggested Reading

Dream Your Way to Success—Trade paper—P407-7
by Nell Kennedy.
The life story of Dr. Paul Yonggi Cho.

•

Solving Life's Problems—Trade paper—P450-7
by Dr. Paul Yonggi Cho.
A guide to personal growth and success.

•

The Fourth Dimension—Trade paper—P380-6
by Dr. Paul Yonggi Cho.
International Bestseller. Secrets for answered prayer and church renewal.

•

The Exploding Church—Trade paper—P299-8
by Tommy Reid with Doug Brendel.
God's infallible formula for church growth.

Subscribe now to the *Logos Journal.* You will enjoy its new emphasis on church growth and successful living, featuring regular articles by Dr. Cho and other leaders of growing churches.

For catalog and *Logos Journal* information write:

Logos Journal—Catalog CG
Box 191
Plainfield, NJ 07061